Incest

Coping with Incest

Incest

Deborah A. Miller, Ph.D.

and Pat Kelly

THE ROSEN PUBLISHING GROUP, INC./NEW YORK

Published in 1992 by The Rosen Publishing Group, Inc.
29 East 21st Street, New York, NY 10010

First Edition

Library of Congress Cataloging-in-Publication Data

Miller, Deborah A.
    Coping with incest / Deborah A. Miller.—1st ed.
      p. cm.
    Includes bibliographical references and index.
    Summary: Discusses the definition of incest, what to do as a
victim or someone who knows a victim, and how to get help.
    ISBN 0-8239-1422-4
    1. Incest—Juvenile literature.   2. Child molesting—Juvenile
literature.   3. Incest victims—Juvenile literature.   4. Sexually
abused children—Juvenile literature. [1. Incest.   2. Child
molesting.   3. Child abuse.]   I. Title.
HQ71.M53   1992
362.7′6—dc20   91-41604
                                             CIP
                                             AC

Manufactured in the United States of America

ABOUT THE AUTHORS ◇

Deborah Miller is an Associate Professor and Health Coordinator at the College of Charleston, Charleston, South Carolina. She teaches a variety of sexuality courses, ranging from such subjects as "Sexual Behavior and Relationships" to "Sexuality Education: Theory and Practice."

Dr. Miller has published twenty research articles, written a student workbook entitled *Dimensions of Human Sexuality* and *Coping with Your Sexual Orientation*, and conducted numerous teacher training programs and workshops on the subject.

As an undergraduate at the University of Illinois, she spent a year in Cologne, Germany, as a foreign exchange student. She completed her Ph.D. at the University of Oregon in 1982 and in 1985 was recognized as one of the Outstanding Young Women of America.

Her interests include the mountains, walking on the beach, and caring for her two miniature dachshunds, Buffie and Schnaupps. She is a music minister at St. Joseph's church, where she sings and plays the guitar.

Pat Kelly works for the South Carolina Governor's Workforce Initiative under the auspices of Trident Technical College in Charleston. Her job is to assist adults in improving their basic reading, writing, and math skills at their job sites.

Ms. Kelly formerly lived in New York City, where she was employed as a manager for a commercial real estate firm. She moved to South Carolina in 1985 to complete her education, graduating from the College of Charleston in 1989 with a B.A. in History and Political Science.

Over the years she has published a number of articles ranging from fiction to editorials. She lives in Charleston with her husband, two children, and a variety of pets.

Contents

Prelude

Child sexual abuse is defined by the National Center on Child Abuse and Neglect as "contacts or interactions between a child and an adult or a significantly older member of the child's family or a parent figure, in which the child is used for sexual stimulation of the perpetrator or another person." Based on this definition, you may be uncomfortable reading many of the graphic stories in this book. The subject of incest involves sexuality, and we live in a society that does not spend much time talking about sexuality in an open and caring way. That is one of the main reasons incest has been able to happen.

To protect the identities of the people we interviewed for this book, their names, ages, and parts of their family backgrounds have been altered. Therefore the characters are fictitious and should not be associated with anyone who may have the same name.

We hope you will take your time reading this book and digest its contents slowly. The information may not fit your situation at home, but you may recognize a close friend's dilemma. If so, please pass the book on to your friend and ask him or her to read it. If this book describes your own abusive situation, remember that you are not alone and you can survive.

COPING WITH

Incest

CHAPTER ◇ 1

Incest: Society's Secret

O f all of the abuses to which children are subjected,
incest is the one that society least wishes to
discuss. It is difficult for many people to deal with
the fact that some children are sexually abused by their
own relatives. Yet the sexual abuse of children by parents,
grandparents, uncles, cousins, and other family members
occurs every day. It is discomforting to talk about fathers
having sex with their daughters or uncles having sex with
their nephews, or even of grandfathers molesting their
grandchildren. Nevertheless, incest is a very real fact of life
for some children.

Incest can be defined in many ways. The most widely
used and basic definition is "any sexual activity between
family members." Family members can include not only
the immediate family such as mothers, fathers, sisters, and
brothers, but also grandparents, aunts and uncles, cousins,
and steprelatives.

According to Parents United, a California-based

organization founded to help incest victims and their families, one in three girls and one in four boys will be sexually abused by their eighteenth birthday. Many of these children will be abused by members of their own family.

In 1985 the Los Angeles *Times* conducted a national telephone survey to determine how widespread was the sexual abuse of children. The results were published on August 25, 1985, and the numbers were startling. The survey found that at least 22 percent of Americans had been sexually abused as children; that means more than thirty-five million adults. At least one third of these people had never told anyone about the abuse, not even their spouses. Of those who did report the abuse, only 3 percent reported to the police.

The exact number of families affected by incest is unknown. Statistics exist, but most professionals believe that many cases are unreported, which is confirmed by the survey. The reasons are many. Although incest is legally and morally wrong, society is so uncomfortable with the idea of parents performing sex acts on their own children that when we hear about it, we tend to look the other way or try to pretend that it did not happen. In cases where mothers or other female family members sexually abuse relatives, reports are often dismissed as misunderstandings because the female in the household is expected to be physically closer to the children than is the male.

The discomfort of discussing incest also occurs among professional people. Although women do commit incest, it is predominantly a male crime, and until the women's liberation movement most professionals dealing with sexual abuse were men schooled in Freudian psychology. Who was Freud and what impact did he have in the area of incest?

SIGMUND FREUD

Sigmund Freud (1856–1939) is considered a pioneer in developmental psychology. Freud believed that all children have incestuous fantasies and that these fantasies are an important part of human personality development. Freud's Oedipus complex theory stated that every child has a strong desire for the parent of the opposite sex. Freud also believed that if incest does occur it is because the child has a strong desire for it and, in fact, behaves in such a seductive manner as to make it occur. Do you believe that the child is responsible for incest? We hope not! A child is never responsible for an adult's behavior.

It was not until Freud was almost forty that he came to realize that the child is not responsible for incest. He openly recognized that the problems of many of his patients were ". . . connected, not with a mental, but with a physical consequence of sexual abuse." In 1896, Freud also recognized that ". . . children are far oftener exposed to sexual aggression than we should suppose."

Unfortunately, he changed his mind again and went back to his theory that children imagine rather than experience actual sexual abuse. Part of the reason for his change of mind seems to have been unwillingness to come to terms with the fact that so many fathers sexually abuse their children. Ultimately he had to admit having dreams in which he was "overly affectionate" toward his own daughter.

Freud's pioneering work in psychology has been both hailed and criticized by other professionals. His research brought him great fame, but some people believe that the opinions of a famous person are not simply opinions but facts. Many professionals today still report incestuous experiences as fantasies rather than as actual occurrences.

Would it be difficult for you to acknowledge someone's incestuous experience as real? Why, or why not?

Another reason people tend to discount reports of incest is because denial is so prevalent. Often when a child reports sexual abuse by a family member, the rest of the family, especially the abuser, denies that incest is occurring. Even in cases where the evidence has substantiated the report and the abusers have been convicted and sent to jail, many men continue to deny what they have done. Even in prison there are hierarchies according to the type of crime the person has committed. Child abusers are considered to be at the bottom of the ladder, and a man who commits incest with his child is even lower than that.

Sometimes other family members who know what is going on may deny it to the authorities. There are many reasons for this also. Although other members of the family may be aware that something is going on, it is rare that they are actual witnesses to the sexual abuse. When the time comes to verify or deny reports of incest, family members tend to interpret events very differently from one another. The following two instances illustrate how family members internalize and respond differently to incest.

A father who is abusing one of his daughters may be more attentive to her than to her siblings. He may take her places, buy her gifts, or give her special privileges that he does not give to his other children. They may actually be jealous of their sister and resent her special treatment. They may be glad to see her removed from the family simply because they want more of their father's attention.

At other times family members may be so dependent on the offender for financial support that they remain silent.

Their fear of being penniless and homeless outweighs their desire for the sexual abuse to stop. They do not seem to understand how important it is to end it because the sexual abuse is not happening to them.

SEXUAL ABUSE OR SEXUAL CURIOSITY?

Not all forms of sexual activity between family members are considered abusive. Most children are naturally curious. One of the things that they are curious about is anatomical differences. It is common for young brothers and sisters or cousins to "play doctor."

Sexual abuse is *not* the same as sexual curiosity. Sexual abuse can be defined as any activity between an adult (or older person) that is for the sexual gratification of that person whether or not it brings any gratification to the child. The following examples show the difference between curiosity and abuse:

Ellen's Story

Ellen is spending the night at her cousin Sally's house. They are both nine years old and are sharing a bed. As they get ready to go to sleep they talk about growing up, dating, and getting their first periods. Ellen asks Sally if she thinks her breasts are starting to develop. Sally says she doesn't think so. Ellen holds her stomach in as far as she can and pushes her chest out. "Now, see!" Ellen says. "Touch them and you can see that they are getting bigger." Sally runs her hands across Ellen's chest and then across her own. "Well, I don't know," objects Sally. "They don't really feel any different than mine." Both girls begin to giggle and finish dressing for bed.

Chantay's Story

Chantay, three years old, and her brother Aaron, five, come running into the house to get cleaned up. They have just had a mud fight, and both of them are filthy. Their mother puts them in the shower together. Chantay notices for the first time that she does not have a penis. She asks Aaron where hers is. "You don't have one, silly," Aaron tells his sister. "Girls don't have penises. They have vaginas." "What's a bagina?" Chantay asks. "I don't know," says Aaron. Chantay reaches out and touches Aaron's penis. After a few seconds she loses interest and they finish their shower.

Chip's Story

Chip and his brother, Donald, are eleven and thirteen years old respectively. Donald has spent the weekend with their cousin, Howard, who is also thirteen. Donald is eager to show Chip what their cousin has taught him. He takes Chip into his bedroom and shows him how to masturbate. They are both excited and scared at how it makes them feel. What would happen if someone caught them?

Although all of the above examples show children engaging in some type of sexual behavior, none of it could be considered more than normal sexual curiosity. Notice that none of the children involved was threatened or frightened by the other child. All of the children were very close in age, and none of them possessed any power over the other. Have you ever been involved in any type of sexual exploration with a family member? Don't worry, sexual curiosity is a natural part of growing up. However, compare the above examples with these. Which make you feel uncomfortable? Try to figure out why you feel uncomfortable before we give you the reason.

Ellen's Story

Ellen is spending the night at her cousin Sally's house. While she is asleep Sally's sixteen-year-old brother, Marty, comes into the bedroom and crawls into bed next to Ellen. He puts his hand under her nightgown and begins to rub her breasts. Ellen wakes up, startled, and pushes Marty away.

Chantay's Story

Chantay's fifteen-year-old Uncle Dwayne is taking care of her while her parents are at the movies. He decides she needs a bath before getting ready for bed. While she is in the bathtub, Dwayne comes in to wash her back. After he washes her back he starts to wash her stomach. He moves the washcloth down to her legs and begins washing her genitals. He puts his hand in her labia and tells her, "Little girls must be very careful to wash everywhere." "Mommy told me never to let anyone touch me there," Chantay says. "Your mommy told me to give you a bath," Dwayne replies and continues fondling her. Chantay does not know what to do because her parents said that Uncle Dwayne was in charge and that she should do as he said and be a "good girl" while they were out.

Chip's Story

Chip is spending the weekend at his aunt's house. While his aunt is out shopping his Uncle Ted takes him for a walk. When they get to the lake his uncle suggests that they go swimming. "But I don't have a bathing suit," Chip objects. "Men don't need bathing suits," his uncle replies. They both take off their clothes and go swimming. After they get out of the water Ted begins to tell Chip about growing up and being a man. He points to Chip's penis. "Let me show you what you can do with that." Ted takes Chip's penis in his hands and begins to masturbate him. As Chip tries to pull away, his uncle says, "Don't be a baby! Be a man like me."

As you can see, the last three stories have nothing to do with normal sexual curiosity. In each one the young child was uncomfortable with the situation and powerless in trying to deal with someone older. In none of the examples did the child initiate any body contact with the older person. All three children were in a vulnerable position when the older person touched them. Ellen was asleep when Sally's brother crept into her bed. Chantay was in the bathtub when her Uncle Dwayne began to touch her on the pretense of giving her a bath. Chip had been swimming in the nude when his uncle started fondling him. None of the children knew how to say "No" and end the sexual behavior that made them uncomfortable.

This book attempts to answer your questions about inappropriate sexual behavior by a close family member and offer suggestions on what to do and whom to see. It may be painful to read parts of this book, so stop temporarily if it becomes too difficult. But remember that you are not alone; many people around you want to help. We want to help!

The next chapter examines some of the common myths that surround the topic of incest. How many of these myths have you heard before?

CHAPTER 2

Myths Surrounding Incest

There are many misconceptions about incest, and a lack of knowledge can be very dangerous to you. Therefore, to understand the topic better it is essential to dispel the myths. You may have heard other myths, but these are the most common ones.

Myth #1: Most children who report sexual abuse by a parent or relative are actually reporting a fantasy.

Reality: Children seldom lie about sexual abuse. Incest is not a subject that you pick up from your day-to-day experiences outside the home. Although Freud tried to convince himself and others that children have sexual fantasies about their parents, most professionals today recognize that he was incorrect and that reports of sexual abuse are usually true.

Myth #2:   Children who report sexual abuse and then change their mind are just looking for attention.

Reality: Those of you who report sexual abuse and then change your mind may do so for a variety of reasons. First, the adult involved may have convinced you that you should change your mind. Children are naive, and adults can be very persuasive in their arguments. It is not uncommon for the abusive adult to tell you that this is an appropriate way to learn about sex and that your relationship is improved by having sex with each other. Depending on your age, such "logic" makes sense and you may change your story.

Second, you may be afraid of breaking up the family. If the abuser is your father or stepfather he may be the primary source of financial support for your family. He may tell you that he will be sent to jail forever and that you will never see him again. Or he may tell you that the Department of Social Services or some other agency will remove you from your home and you may never see your mother, brothers and sisters, or pets again. This threat of total isolation from your family is devastating, and you may rationalize that you can put up with the abuse as long as your family remains together.

Third, an abused child may fear retaliation from the adult involved. Threats of physical violence against your mother or younger siblings or even cruelty to your pets may change your mind about reporting sexual abuse. The abusive adult may beat you or threaten your life. Most children are very protective of people and things that they love and will endure great physical and emotional pain to protect them. To what lengths would you go to protect members of your family? Now can you understand why you and other abused children might change your stories about sexual abuse at home?

Myth #3:   Incest does not really harm a child.

Reality: We normally think of childhood as a happy, carefree time in which the family meets all our needs. It is a safe environment in which we can grow up slowly and be protected from harm. Incest, however, robs you of a normal childhood. A child whose trust in another relative has been violated frequently becomes withdrawn, nervous, or suspicious of others. You may experience sleep disorders, changes in eating patterns, or pregnancy. In addition, you may have difficulty in school because your mind is preoccupied with what is happening at home. You may become truant or, as a last resort, run away. Although not everyone who has been abused by a relative experiences the same feelings, studies of incest victims have shown that most have problems that they carry with them into adulthood.

Let's look at some startling facts about the victims of incest and then see if we can still believe that "incest does not really harm a child." Eighty percent of sexually abusive fathers were sexually abused children. Eighty percent of prostitutes were incest victims during childhood. Seventy percent of drug abusers were sexually molested by family members. Could there possibly be a link between these "victims" and their current life-styles? Many researchers say yes, that adult survivors may exhibit inappropriate behaviors. We shall examine that phenomenon in greater detail in a later chapter.

Before we move on to the next myth, we want to put your mind at ease. None of this means that if you are a victim of incest you will become a sex abuser, drug user, or prostitute. It simply means that a majority of sex abusers, drug users, and prostitutes (male and female) were sexually abused as children. It also means that incest is very harmful to children; it robs them of their normal childhood and, in some cases, their normal adulthood as well.

Myth #4:   Incest is not a crime unless physical force is used.

Reality: Many cases of incest do not involve any physical force. Abusers may offer friendship, time alone with them, and material objects to gain your trust and endear them to you. This type of emotional manipulation is calculated and very difficult for a child to deal with. You do not have the life skills even to realize that you are being used when the abuser employs such tactics.

It does not matter whether you freely engage in the sexual activity. Because of your age, you cannot give informed consent. All sexual activity between an adult and a child should be considered self-serving for the adult. Whether or not physical force is used, incest is *always* a crime.

Myth #5:   Incest occurs only in lower-income families.

Reality: It is easier to believe that incest occurs only among the poor or the less educated, but in reality it does not discriminate. Incest occurs in all geographic areas, at all socioeconomic levels, at all educational levels, in all religious groups, and in all races and cultures. From research, however, we can describe the potentially incestuous household and identify children who are at risk of being sexually abused by family members. Chapter 4 describes in greater detail who commits incest.

Myth #6: For incest to occur, there must be sexual intercourse.

Reality: Although intercourse often occurs in an incestuous relationship, most cases do not involve intercourse. Sometimes the adult stops at fondling the genitals or breasts and exhibitionism. Sometimes an inadvertent interruption occurs such as someone's coming into the house or room unexpectedly. You may have cried out, "No," "Stop," or "You're hurting me!" Whether or not there is intercourse, any sexual activity for the gratification of the adult is considered sexual abuse.

Myth #7: Only girls are victims of incest.

Reality: Although the vast majority of incest victims are girls, many boys are victims also. The myth stems largely from the fact that boys rarely report sexual abuse. It is estimated that 27 percent of all female children and 16 percent of all male children in the United States are victims of sexual abuse. These estimates include both incest and abusive sexual activity. In his book *Hidden Victims: The Sexual Abuse of Children*, R. Geiser found that 97 percent of the offenders were males and 92 percent of the victims of reported incest were females.

The reasons for underreporting by boys are not clearly understood. Several possible reasons have been identified in the literature: (1) it is suspected that boys fear the reaction of their peers more than girls if the abuse is made public; (2) boys have more freedom and independence than girls, and they fear losing that freedom and independence;

(3) boys may fear more violent reprisals from the abuser than do girls; and (4) society expects boys to be able to fight their way out of any situation. Therefore, the pressure on a boy to have been able to stop the abuse is overwhelming. If you were a boy who had been sexually abused, whom would you confide in? What do you think your friends would say or think?

Myth #8: Boys who are victims of incest become homosexuals.

Reality: Fear of being identified or labeled homosexual prevents many boys from reporting sexual abuse. Your sexual orientation has nothing to do with incest. Despite all the research into sexual orientation, little can be said with certainty regarding the development of heterosexuality, bisexuality, or homosexuality. Over the years many theories have been proposed to explain sexual orientation, but none of them have held that if you are a victim of incest you will become homosexual. You do not choose to participate in incest any more than you choose your sexual orientation.

Myth #9: Only stepfathers abuse their children.

Reality: Statistics show that you are more likely to be sexually abused by a stepfather or surrogate father (a live-in boyfriend or lover of your mother's) than a biological father, but reports of sexual abuse by other relatives are also common. It is thought that stepfather-stepdaughter incest is as much as five times more common than father-daughter incest. Why do you think that would be true?

Stepfathers seem to abuse their stepchildren more readily than biological fathers because the incest taboo is not as strong since they are not "blood" relatives. Also, stepfathers may have fewer paternal, protective instincts since they have not known the child from infancy. Far less common but equally damaging is grandfather-granddaughter, sibling, mother-son, stepmother-stepson, and grandmother-grandson incest. We have no accurate statistics on the frequency of these types of incest. Although police reports, court records, and protective agencies have reported that the overwhelming majority of abusers are men, women are also capable of sexually abusing children.

Myth #10:   Fathers have sex with their children because their wives won't have sex with them.

Reality: No matter what the relationship between your parents, you are not expected to fulfill their sexual needs. Incest occurs even when a husband and his wife have a sexual relationship. Although incest involves sexual activity, incest itself is not about sex. It is about power over another person.

Fearing rejection from his wife and confident that his daughter will not be in a position to reject him, the father turns to his emotionally dependent daughter to fulfill his sexual needs. Note that we did not say that his wife rejected him, but rather that he *feared* rejection by his wife! As you can see, the incestuous father has power over his dependent daughter.

Myth #11:   Incest occurs only once or twice.

Reality: This myth is discredited by research, which indicates that the average duration of the experience is five years. Although victims may range from several months old to late teenage, studies have determined that the median age of your first encounter was probably between six and eleven years old. In addition, you may not have been the only victim in your family. Your abuser may have told you that if you remained silent about the abuse he would not harm your younger sisters and brothers. Unfortunately, we know that often he used that same line on your siblings, and each of you tried to protect each other by remaining silent. Ultimately, you *all* may have been abused while you tried to protect each other. You must have loved your siblings very much to have remained silent so long.

Myth #12:   Sexual assault by a stranger is more traumatic for a child than incest.

Reality: The emotional trauma that you may experience as a result of a sexual encounter with someone you trusted is far more devastating than that you may experience at the hands of a stranger. While you were growing up you were warned by your parents and teachers to be wary of strangers who might harm you. Few educational programs talked about personal body safety and what to do when someone you knew touched you in a way that made you uncomfortable. Physical wounds heal quickly, especially when you are young. Psychological wounds produce deep scars that take professional counseling to heal. And even then, overcoming incest is a very painful task that you must accomplish by yourself. Fortunately, loving friends and family members may offer you the support that was missing during the long years that you were a victim.

Myth #13:   Incest would not occur if mothers stayed at home.

Reality: It is important not to blame mothers for the sexual exploitation of their daughters. As D.E.H. Russell points out, such blaming assumes that "daughters must be chaperoned in their own homes in order to be safe." Many incidents of incest do occur while mothers and siblings are at home. If the abusive adult is intent on exploiting you, he will find an opportunity when you are vulnerable and least able to resist. Remember, incest does not have to occur in the home. It may occur in a car, his office, a hotel room, or any other place where the abuser feels he is in control.

All these myths are dangerous to believe, but there is one more myth that is perhaps the most harmful. Do you have any idea what it might be?

Myth #14:   If the child does not resist the relative's sexual advances, the child is just as responsible as the adult.

Reality: Children do not resist the advances of older persons for a variety of reasons. You have been taught to obey your parents and to respect your relatives without question. Adults are in positions of authority and power, and it is not easy for you to challenge them. Also, your family rules may be based on the philosophy that "children may be seen, but not heard." In such case you are powerless.

It is a fact of life that adults are bigger and stronger than children. How difficult would it be for an adult, either male or female, to overpower a six- or seven-year-old? Even if you tried to resist, you are no match for any adult. Have you ever used physical force or tried to restrain someone? If you have, odds are you restrained someone who was weaker or younger, someone whom you knew you could overpower. Why didn't you try to restrain someone who was bigger than you?

Sexual abuse often occurs in homes where physical abuse also exists. Even though the offender may not have used physical force against you, if violence was a factor in your household you had every reason to believe it would be used against you if you tried to resist. Sometimes to preserve our life we must submit to one type of physical abuse to prevent a more violent abuse. You are not alone if you submitted to incest. At least you survived the ordeal; sadly, some victims do not.

Some children never have a chance to resist. It is not uncommon for sexual abuse to begin when the victim is asleep. It is difficult to resist something when you are unaware that it is happening.

Many children are too young to resist. In Los Angeles County, California, sexual abuse was most common between the ages of two to four. As we mentioned earlier, even infants have been victims of sexual abuse. The younger you were when the incest began, the less capable you were of resisting the incestuous adult.

Another reason identified for children not to resist is economic dependence. Children do not have the means to support themselves, and it is perfectly normal for them to rely on their parents for food, clothing, and shelter. Although leaving home to avoid sexual abuse is a viable alternative for older children, it may not have been a viable alternative for you. What kind of job could you have held at seven, eight, or nine years of age? Where would you have lived except on the street? You didn't have many options.

Sometimes children do not resist because of nonphysical threats. The abusive parent may threaten to throw you out of the house or revoke an important privilege if you do not submit to his or her advances. You may have felt absolutely powerless at the time and believed that you had no choice but to submit. Depending on the threat and its consequences, submission may have been your only choice.

Some children do not resist because they do not know what is happening. The younger the child, the less outside contacts he or she has. With nothing to compare against, you had no way of knowing that most children do not experience sexual activity with a relative.

Countless interviews with children have determined that they did not resist because they truly loved the offender. In many cases the sexually abusive behavior was the only affection or attention they received. In your situation you may not have resisted because you felt that some affection was better than none at all. Or you may even have rationalized that the sexual behavior was "accidental" and would never happen again.

Are there any other circumstances that would encourage you to submit to an adult's sexual advances? The answer is, of course! You are emotionally, physically, and economically dependent on your parents and numerous other family members. Any circumstance that potentially threatens those relationships could lead to your submission. Sexual abuse is not something you expect, nor is it something you desire. Unfortunately, it is sometimes something that you must endure.

As you continue reading this book, you need to know that the cycle of violence can be stopped. Not every adult is sexually abusive. In fact, most adults care about your welfare and want to help. Now that we have dispelled some of the myths associated with incest, let's look at the incest taboo.

CHAPTER 3

The Incest Taboo

The taboo against nuclear-family incest is universal with few exceptions. Although there are some examples of socially sanctioned brother/sister incest, there are almost no examples of parent/child incest. Even in the play *Oedipus*, although Oedipus marries his mother he does not know that she is his mother; he had been removed from her as an infant.

The literature on incest provides only two examples of incestuous societies. Let's look at those societies and see why and under what circumstances incest was acceptable.

The Hippopotamus Hunters.   More than a century ago in Africa, the people of a society of aborigines believed that their hunts would be more successful if they had sexual intercourse with their daughters just before the hunt. Having an incestuous relationship with his daughter would kill something within the father, making him a murderer and allowing him to join the hunt without fear. Even though incest was encouraged before the hunt, it was intended to destroy the father's humanity to make him as fierce as the animal he hunted. Before the hunt, however, incest was considered an intolerable act.

Ancient Egypt. The ruling families of ancient Egypt permitted brothers and sisters to marry to preserve the royal lineage. Few people stop to think that Cleopatra married her half-brother, Ptolemy. Certain prohibitions were observed, however. A brother and sister could marry only if they had different mothers. Only members of the royal family were allowed to engage in this practice; incest among the common members of society was illegal.

All societies today strictly forbid incest, some even under penalty of death. Can you think of any negative consequences for the individual or for society if incest were "normal" sexual behavior? Biological, sociological, and psychological consequences are associated with incest. We shall examine these individually.

THE BIOLOGICAL CONSEQUENCES

When a man and woman engage in sexual intercourse, their offspring receives genes from each of them. Normally, the child ends up with the strongest or "dominant" genes, which determine the child's eye and hair color, body build, and even health status. Reproduction between closely related family members, however, tends to bring out the worst genetic combinations by allowing the pairing of two weaker or mutant recessive genes. These genes might not have appeared if the mating had occurred between two unrelated individuals. The following examples illustrate mutant recessive genes.

The Hapsburg Chin

Charles II of Spain was the last of the direct line of the German princely house of Hapsburg. Generations of marriages between Hapsburgs, although not between parents and children or brothers and sisters, had passed down the "Hapsburg chin." Charles's chin was so pronounced that as he grew older he was unable to eat and died prematurely. If close family members had not married for generations, Charles might have lived longer. Instead, the mutant recessive genes produced the "Hapsburg chin," which contributed to his early death.

The Louisiana Cajuns

Recently, in Louisiana, medical experts learned of a recurrence of Tay-Sachs disease, a disorder that they had believed almost eradicated in the United States. The death rate of Cajun children was higher than the national average. Researchers finally determined that the social isolation of the community had left the Cajuns vulnerable to the disease. The Cajuns are a close-knit community; they tend to marry other Cajuns, and everyone is related to almost everyone else. Like the "Hapsburg chin," the Tay-Sachs gene is a recessive gene. Although the Cajuns were not engaging in incestuous relationships, the closeness of the community increased the odds of two people with the same recessive gene marrying and passing that gene on to a child. The chance for recessive genes to dominate was greater than in a community where people were not so closely related.

THE SOCIOLOGICAL CONSEQUENCES

In the 1950s sociologist Talcott Parsons published an article entitled "The Incest Taboo in Relation to Social Structure and the Socialization of the Child." Dr. Parsons agreed that the incest taboo was important in preventing the passing on of mutant recessive genes, but he thought it also helped to strengthen the family and the society. Parsons explained that enforcement of the incest taboo made family roles better defined and exclusive and enabled the family to function more efficiently. In other words, an efficient family consisted of a mother, a father, daughters, and sons. The wife and husband also had female/male roles, while the children were considered dependent. Fathers and daughters (or mothers and sons) could not have sexual relationships without upsetting the balance of the family. Violating the incest taboo created confusion regarding the role of each family member.

The incest taboo also strengthened society by obliging family members to find their mates outside of the nuclear family. Thus, not only were new families formed but also social ties between families were created. What would your family be like if you had no aunts or uncles or cousins?

THE PSYCHOLOGICAL CONSEQUENCES

Perhaps the most important reason for the taboo is the long-term psychological impact that incest has on the victim. Incest violates the natural dependency relationship between parent and child. You depend on your parents for unconditional love, security, and guidance. Incest disrupts your emotional development because of the confusion of the relationships.

An incestuous household is one filled with secrets,

where family members do not really talk to one another. Instead, you grow up feeling confused, angry, isolated, and afraid. There is increasing evidence that the scars of incest follow you into adulthood. Female incest survivors often have difficulty forming intimate adult relationships, especially with men. It is also common for incest survivors to experience low self-esteem, depression, guilt, shame, addictive behaviors such as drug and alcohol abuse or easting disorders, and a sense of isolation.

You're probably wondering if you have to be an adult before you experience these feelings. Of course not! You may be experiencing them right now. As you continue reading this book, you may begin to understand yourself and your family more with every chapter. The isolation that you have felt is common among incest victims, but you are not alone in your feelings or your struggles. The next chapter profiles who commits incest and why.

CHAPTER ◇ 4

Who Commits Incest and Why

Although everyone is potentially capable of violating the incest taboo, most people do not. Incest offenders come from all backgrounds, all economic strata, and all occupations, races, and religions. Some offenders are ministers; some are lawyers; some are teachers, doctors, electricians, welders, mailmen, secretaries. Some offenders have problems with alcohol and drug abuse, but others do not. Many offenders were themselves sexually abused as children, but some were not. A group of people who are considered at greater risk of becoming offenders are those who were themselves abused. Although that in no way excuses their behavior, it offers a partial explanation. Not all sexually abused children grow up to be child abusers themselves, but some do.

Sometimes circumstances lend themselves to potentially abusive situations. When a parent is predisposed toward committing sexual abuse, the opportunity increases in a household where the father and child are often alone for long periods of time. The mother may be bedridden, in the hospital, at work, or dead. Mother/child incest is more likely to occur in a household where the father is missing.

Another circumstance that lends itself to the occurrence of incest is the period of time immediately following a stressful event. The loss of a job, a terrible accident, or the death of a spouse or other relative may result in the father's being in a depressed or anxious state. If he turns to alcohol or drugs for consolation, the possibility for abuse increases.

We have mentioned that if the father was sexually abused as a child, the potential for his abusing his own children increases, especially if he has not had counseling. Also women who have been victims of incest frequently marry abusive men, thus increasing the potential for the "cycle of incest" to continue.

Although no family is immune from incest, some general types of men appear more likely to be sexually abusive under certain circumstances. Let's examine these personalities and see how they affect the children in the family. Maybe you can identify with some of these children, maybe not. Your own situation may be better or worse than theirs. At least you know you are not alone in your feelings. Children from all walks of life are secretly dealing with the incest taboo. Researchers have identified the following profiles in abusers.

THE DEPENDENT PARENT

The dependent father seems to feel sorry for himself much of the time. He is unable (or unwilling) to do things for himself, and so he depends on everyone in the household to take care of him. He is immature, has few friends, and cannot deal effectively with stress.

Kris's Story

Kris's mother died in a car accident when Kris was eleven years old. For weeks after the funeral her father just sat around the house and cried. Kris began taking on all the household chores that her mother had done. She cleaned, shopped, and prepared dinner for her father. She washed and ironed his clothes and even woke him up for work. Although Kris missed her mother very much, she felt that she and her father were growing closer every day. He was always complimenting her on how nice the house looked and how delicious the dinners were. "I don't know what I'd do without you. You take such good care of me," he often said to her.

Kris's father sometimes crawled into bed with her when he was feeling particularly lonely and missing his wife. She and her father would cuddle for a while, and then he would go back to his own bed. One night Kris fell asleep while her father was still in her bed. She woke up when she felt him rubbing her breasts. She didn't say anything to her father but got up and went into the living room to sleep on the couch. Besides leaving the bedroom, what more could Kris have done?

Ana Consuela's Story

Ana Consuela's father lost his job when the company he worked for went out of business. Because of the recession he had difficulty finding employment in his field, and he became very depressed. Her mother found a night job at a local factory. She left for work at four in the afternoon and returned home a little after midnight each night. When Ana Consuela came home from school, she would fix dinner for her father and do the laundry and the cleaning.

Her father said he was very proud of the way his "little girl" took care of him.

One evening after dinner Ana Consuela's father started to cry. He had been turned down for another job that day and had stopped at a bar for a few drinks before coming home. He told Ana Consuela how upsetting it was to have her mother as the chief breadwinner. He felt like a failure. Ana Consuela put her arms around him to comfort him. He hugged her back, and after a few minutes he started kissing her. Ana Consuela felt uncomfortable about the way he kissed her, but she didn't want to upset him so she let him kiss her again. What would you have done in her situation?

In both of these examples the mothers were absent. Both Kris and Ana Consuela took over household chores that had been done by their mothers. In our society we frequently assign household and child-care chores to daughters, in effect making them into "little mothers" themselves.

Both Kris and Ana Consuela became the "little mothers" of the household, thus blurring the boundaries between parent and child. It is important to remember that simply taking on household responsibilities does not automatically determine that a daughter will become a victim of incest.

In both of these examples, the fathers were dependent on their daughters to care for them. They seemed unable to cope with the realities of life in a mature, responsible manner. Many men lose their jobs, lose their wives, and do not confuse their daughters with their wives. Nevertheless, in men who are predisposed to commit incest those circumstances tend to increase the possibility. Ana Consuela's father increased the likelihood of incest by drinking. Men who are convicted of sexual abuse often blame it on alcohol. But although alcohol abuse is a factor in many abusive households, just as often it is not. Alcohol lowers a person's inhibitions, making it easier to do things he or she would not ordinarily do. But alcohol itself does not make people do things. It only makes it easier for potential abusers to deny responsibility for their behavior. Many people drink but do not then engage in incestuous activities with their children.

Although it is usually men who commit incest, women may also be involved in incestuous relationships. Usually the incestuous mother is a woman very much like the dependent father. She always feels sorry for herself, she seems unable to do things for herself, and she has difficulty with mature male/female relationships.

Sergei's Story

Sergei's father had abandoned the family when Sergei was three years old. He did not remember much about his dad, but his mother often told him what an awful person his father had been. Sergei was sorry that his dad had left, but he also felt helpless about how sad his mother seemed all the time. His mother said that he was all she had left and that she never wanted him to leave her. She said he was the man of the house. Whenever Sergei took a bath, his mother came in to wash him. Even when he was eight years old she still came into the bathroom to wash his back. Sometimes at night his mother asked Sergei to come and sleep in her bed. When he objected, "I'm a big boy, and big boys sleep in their own beds," his mother would cry and say that he didn't love her anymore. Then he would be sorry that he had upset her and would crawl into bed with her. His mother would cuddle him and rub his back and sometimes stroke his penis. All this intimacy made Sergei feel loved and happy.

When Sergei became a teenager and interested in girls, his mother told him that most girls were "no good" and that no one would ever love him as she did. She withheld messages when girls called him on the phone. Every night she made up another excuse for him to sleep in her bed: She was afraid of a thunderstorm, or she heard someone outside, or she was very lonely.

One night Sergei woke up to feel his mother kissing his penis. He was embarrassed because he had an erection and did not know what to do, so he pretended to be asleep. The next morning he felt ashamed and could not look at his mother. Sergei felt that he was to blame and that he should have stopped her. How did his mother coerce him into sleeping in her bed? Have you ever fallen into that trap?

Sergei's mother is an example of a dependent parent just like Kris's and Ana Consuela's fathers. She made Sergei feel guilty whenever he wanted to do something on his own. Even when he became a teenager she manipulated him. When he started to show an interest in girls she treated him like a husband. In incestuous households there is role confusion. Children are treated like adults and children at the same time. Just like the fathers of Kris and Ana Consuela, Sergei's mother took advantage of his unconditional love for her.

THE TYRANT

Another type associated with incest is the tyrant. The tyrannical father wants total control over everything and everyone in the household. In such a paternalistic family you are taught to obey your father at all times and to expect punishment for any sign of disobedience. You are taught that whatever your father does is acceptable and must not be questioned. The tyrant also abuses his wife and has bullied her so much that she does not interfere with his actions.

Lois's Story

One day while Lois was at school, her father searched her room and found a pamphlet on sex education in one of the dresser drawers. He frequently went through his daughter's things to make sure she was not doing anything he would disapprove of.

When Lois came home he showed her the pamphlet and demanded to know where it had come from. She told him she had received it during health class. Then he asked why she needed information about sex unless she was already having sex. Lois began to cry. She said she was not having sex, and she repeated that she had been given the pamphlet by her teacher. Her father asked why she needed information on sex from a stranger. She explained that all the ninth graders had received the pamphlet and that her mother had said it was all right to go to the class. With that, her father slapped her and told her that sex was something to be learned at home and not in school. He then shouted that her mother was too stupid to know anything about sex education, that *he* would show her what sex was all about.

Lois's mother heard the shouting and came to see what was going on. She started toward her daugher, but her husband pushed her against the wall and told her to get out and mind her own business if she knew what was good for her. Then he dragged Lois into her bedroom, locked the door, and raped her. While he was doing that, Lois could hear her mother in the next room crying.

Lois's father is typical of the way a tyrant behaves. He allowed no privacy and searched her room while she was not there. He wasn't looking for anything specific, just something. He physically abused both Lois and her mother and refused to listen to anything they had to say. In such a household there is little anyone can do that the father thinks is right. He makes the rules and the decisions for everyone. It is not uncommon for this type of father to engage in sexual activity with his daughter under the pretense of sex education. That is not sex education, however. It is a form of sexual abuse.

THE SOCIOPATH

The sociopath, someone who has trouble functioning in society, represents another personality prone to incest. He sees the outside world as a hostile enemy. He is frequently brutal and violent, often sadistic, and may have engaged in criminal behavior. Notice how the sociopath affected Mark's life in the next story.

Mark's Story

Mark lived with his parents and his older sister and younger brother until he was twelve years old and was arrested for setting fires. Because of his age, his case was referred to the juvenile authorities, who began an investigation of his background. Mark's father owned a large construction company, which was doing quite well. It was frequently charged with violating safety standards, but nothing had ever been proved. The family lived in an expensive home on the outskirts of town. Mark's mother did not work outside the home and seldom left the house because her husband had forbidden her to learn to drive. If she wanted to go anywhere she had to wait for her husband to take her.

All the children were doing poorly in school and had no relationships with any of their peers. Because their house was in an isolated area, the family had few neighbors who could give the investigators any information. The juvenile counselor assigned to Mark's case was aware that setting fires was not uncommon among male incest victims, so he gently questioned Mark about his home life. The counselor turned out to be correct. Not only had the father been abusing Mark but also his other two children. Mark told the counselor that his abuse had begun when he was seven years old. He had gone to a friend's house after school without asking permission because his father never let any of the children visit with anyone. When his friend's parents had dropped Mark at home, his father had been waiting. First he had beaten Mark with a belt, then he had forced him to perform oral sex. After that, whenever Mark's father wanted to punish him, he made him engage in sexual activity.

Mark said that his mother knew what had been going on but that his father frequently beat her also, and she was too afraid to say anything to anyone. His sister had run away from home twice, but each time his father had caught her, and her punishment had been the same as Mark's. Mark said his father always ordered him and his mother and brother to sit in the living room while he punished his daughter so they could all hear her crying and begging him to stop. Mark began setting fires as a way to get attention when his father began punishing his younger brother in the same way. Besides setting fires, what else could Mark have done? Why do you think Mark's mother remained in such an abusive relationship?

Mark's father sexually and physically abused all three of his children. He also abused his wife. He was violent and made the others listen while he sodomized his daughter. He kept his family isolated and made his wife a virtual prisoner. Mark's father damaged the lives of his entire family in a brutal, sadistic manner. Although his construction company was doing well, he appeared to be engaged in practices that could endanger the lives of other people. Frequently the sociopath is a dangerous person, and the only way to prevent him from hurting other people is to put him in jail.

Ute's Story

Ute lived with her parents and two younger brothers. Although she loved her mother and her brothers, she thought her father was crazy and should be locked up. He was always finding an excuse to take off his belt and beat her and her brothers. Although he had a good job, he liked to brag about how he managed to score a few extra bucks by repainting stolen cars. Ute's mother was an extremely nervous woman, afraid of her husband's temper and always waiting for the police to knock on the door.

Ute's father had been sexually abusing her since she was five years old. He said that if she ever told her mother he would kill her. She believed him because he had killed her pet kitten after it had scratched him. When Ute turned fourteen a boy in her class called to ask her to go to the movies. Her father became very angry, called her "whore" and "slut," and accused her of having had sex with the boy.

He said that the boy was never to call again. When Ute was fifteen, she ran away from home to get away from her father.

Ute's father was physically and sexually abusive. His behavior was violent and controlling. Killing a kitten because it scratches is like killing a dog because it barks. Everyone knows that kittens scratch when they are playing. When a boy called Ute for a date, her father became verbally abusive because he was jealous. Fathers are not normally jealous of their daughters' boyfriends. Although Ute's father had never been arrested, he was engaged in illegal activities.

Ute was unable to avoid her father's sexual abuse when she was five. Not only was she too young to know what was going on, but she had every reason to believe that he would kill her if she told anyone. Would killing her father solve the problem? Unfortunately, it would compound the problem even further. Violence is never a solution, and it usually makes matters worse. Besides running away, what else could Ute have done? How could her brothers have helped? What role did her mother play in this situation?

THE PEDOPHILE

The pedophile, someone who is sexually attracted to young children, represents another incestuous profile. He generally begins abusing his children when they are quite young. Pedophiles do not usually limit their activities to their own children, but abuse children outside the home as well. It is not unusual for a pedophile to marry a woman with young children simply to obtain access to the children. Unlike the other types of personalities described, the pedophile does not need emotional trauma or excessive stress to trigger incestuous behavior. He slowly introduces his son or daughter to a sexual relationship.

Tiffany's Story

Tiffany was two years old when her mother married Sam. Tiffany liked Sam because he played with her and took her places. He liked to tickle her and wrestle around the floor with her. Sam made Tiffany feel good because he was always ready with a hug. When he gave her a bath he always put in lots of bubble bath so that it looked like a tub full of snow. Sam never touched Tiffany in a sexual way at first, because he wanted her to get comfortable with him. Gradually bath time progressed from blowing bubbles at each other to Sam washing Tiffany. Because he had approached her slowly, Tiffany did not feel nervous when he bathed her. Whenever he touched her labia, Sam would tickle her at the same time. By the time Tiffany was six she was having oral sex with Sam and enjoying it.

When Sam first came into Tiffany's life she was too young to suspect anything. Sam won her confidence by playing games with her and paying attention to her in non-threatening ways. By introducing her to sex slowly he was able to make Tiffany feel comfortable with him so that when he began to abuse her sexually she was unaware that she was being abused.

The dependent parent, the tyrant, the sociopath, and the pedophile are some of the personalities associated with incest. There are many other types as well. A common theme for all of them is that they have difficulty dealing with adult relationships.

Although society tends to view incest offenders as "sick," the fact is that most are aware that what they are doing is wrong. They *choose* to engage in incestuous behavior. One of the responsibilities of adulthood is self-control. Most adults do not steal something just because they want it. Most adults do not decide to take several days off from work just because they feel like it.

One of the reasons incest is so hard to detect is that offenders usually do not display any extraordinary habits in day-to-day life. They hold jobs; they pay their bills on time; they go to religious services. It is only at home that they exhibit abusive behavior. They abuse their power and position in the family by taking advantage of your powerlessness, dependence, trust, ignorance, and love.

You are not born with the knowledge that incest is wrong or that when an adult has sex with you he or she is committing a crime. Victims of incest frequently are not aware that normal families do not have sex with one another. You learn this when you go to school and begin interacting with other children. The incest offender is aware that his or her behavior is abusive and criminal and usually tries to limit your outside contacts to avoid exposure.

Another way incest offenders deal with their abusive behavior is to pretend that their actions are really something else. See if any of these excuses have been used in your family. If they have, remember that the adult is always responsible for his or her behavior, not you!

SHIFTING THE BLAME

It is not uncommon for adults who have been discovered in incestuous relationships to deny responsibility for their actions. Sometimes they blame alcohol or drug use.

Sometimes they blame the victim. Although aware that their behavior is wrong, they attempt to rationalize their incestuous relationship to relieve their own guilt.

Some fathers who have committed incest have tried to rationalize it by saying that incest is better than adultery, that at least they kept their sexual activity "in the family." They argue that they were not getting the sexual attention they needed from their wife and needed to satisfy their sex drive somehow. By turning to their daughter instead of someone outside the family, they tell themselves that somehow they have not been unfaithful to their spouse.

The fact is that not only have they committed adultery, but they have engaged in a serious form of child abuse. Not only has an incestuous father violated the bond of trust between husband and wife, but also that between father and mother. Even more, he has violated the bond of trust between parent and child. Legally and morally, adultery is defined as having sex with someone other than your spouse. There are no exceptions for having sex with other family members.

Some fathers have said that they had sex with their daughter to cure a venereal disease. Back in the Victorian era men tried to justify having sex with other women by the same rationale; they claimed that having sex with a virgin would cure their disease.

Of course, the only way to cure a venereal disease is by medical treatment. The only thing accomplished by such a father having sex with his daughter is to pass the disease on to her. How do you think a myth like that ever got started?

Another feeble explanation that some fathers have used is trying to prevent an already promiscuous daughter from having sex outside the family. Statistics on reported incest show that although one result of being an incest victim may be promiscuity, most girls are promiscuous neither before nor during the time that their father is abusing them. Even if you were willingly having sex with someone, that in no way justifies your father's having sex with you. The normal reaction for a father who wishes to prevent a daughter's sexual activity is to stop her from seeing the person or to restrict her to the house. No responsible parent engages in sexual activity with his or her own child. Supportive, loving, and functional families set reasonable guidelines in dating relationships; therefore promiscuity is rarely an issue. How would you handle a promiscuous daughter? Would your guidelines be the same for a son?

Still another excuse given by convicted incestuous fathers is that they were providing their daughters with sex education. Sex education is taught through lecture and simulation, not demonstration. Schools have sex education curricula that are age-appropriate. Libraries have many books on the subject. Parents who guide their children *explain* sex; they do not demonstrate it. Although sex knowledge ought to be learned at home, it frequently is not. In incestuous households sex is rarely discussed. Instead, it is used as a weapon for personal gratification and control. Abusive fathers who rationalize their behavior as education are unable to explain why the lessons have to be kept secret. If you are receiving secret sexuality lessons at home, be sure to tell an adult whom you trust. Sexuality education is an essential part of your overall education, and sharing such information is a healthy part of growing up.

For decades abusive fathers have blamed their incestuous behavior on their wives' lack of sexual response. You should never be used as a sex surrogate. The problems that may exist between a husband and wife cannot be solved by involving you. You have the right to decide with whom you will be sexually active. Parents do not have the right to make that decision for you.

Males frequently try to justify abusive sexual behavior as a matter of being unable to control themselves. One of the signs of a mature adult is self-control. Adults are responsible for their actions, no matter what the supposed provocation. An adult who cannot control his sexual impulses needs therapy and must be held responsible.

Last, but not least, some incestuous fathers have said that they were seduced by their daughters. When you behave in a seductive manner, a responsible adult guides you and explains the inappropriateness of your behavior. Sexual relationships between adults and children, their own or anyone else's, are against the law in every state. All fifty states have ruled that the adult is responsible for his or her own actions. You are never to blame and should not feel guilty when the incestuous behavior is revealed.

This chapter has attempted to describe who commits incest and why. The next chapter focuses on the incestuous household and identifies who is at risk. Before reading it, try to describe the incestuous household. Then compare your own list with the material in the chapter.

CHAPTER ◇ 5

The Family

Although no family can be guaranteed to be free from sexual abuse, some families appear to be more at risk than others. Information from reported incest crimes provides some general indicators of potential at-risk families. As you read this chapter you may discover that your family is at risk. Keep in mind that in later chapters we shall discuss what you can do if you are at risk.

WHO IS AT RISK?

Intergenerational Abuse

Families in which one or more parent was a victim of sexual abuse are at greater risk than those in which neither parent was sexually abused as a child. Statistics show that women who were molested by their fathers tend to marry abusive men. In part that is because these women, who generally have had no counseling, continue to suffer the psychological damage of childhood incest. Your mother may have low self-esteem and little assertiveness and may accept continued abuse rather than challenge your father.

41

Some men who have been sexually abused as children abuse children themselves, especially if they have not received counseling as a result of their childhood experiences. In part, they learned that fathers can demonstrate their power by exploiting others more vulnerable and less powerful and get away with it. Your father may also suffer from low self-esteem and have learned to try to counteract feelings of powerlessness by aggressive behavior. This may partially explain why your father is abusive toward you.

Adults who were abused as children and were supported in disclosing the fact by the nonoffending parent or other family members often received counseling. They are at much less risk for abusing their own children than those who did not receive counseling.

Stepfamilies

Having a stepfather increases the risk of incestuous experiences. Because your stepfather is not a blood relative, the incest taboo does not appear to be as strong as it is in a family where the biological father is present. In addition, the mother may feel more financially dependent because of having someone other than the biological father support her children. At the same time it should be understood that in some stepfamilies the mother is less emotionally attached because she is aware that she has survived the disruption of a first marriage.

One-Parent Families

In situations where only one parent is in the home the potential for sexual abuse increases, especially if the parent is the father. Being the only adult in the household obviates having to explain his or her behavior to any other adult. In addition, there is more opportunity, as you and the adult are often alone together. In families separated by divorce, sexual assaults by abusive fathers often occur during visitation times. That does *not* mean, however, that your father will abuse you at such times. It simply means that in some families it may be a vulnerable time. If it is so for you, you have the right to say, "I don't want to be alone with him or her."

Large Families

Being a member of a large family also increases the risk of an incestuous experience, especially if the family members do not get along well. A study of fathers jailed for incest showed that they had an average of slightly over five children. A large household, by its very size, is more chaotic than a small one. There is less privacy, more opportunity for accidental intimacy, and less supervision. The mother is frequently more tired because of the corresponding demands on her time. The frustration level is frequently greater than in smaller families. If the household members are prone to physical violence, the possibility for sexual abuse also increases.

Substance Abusers

Being in a family where someone abuses alcohol or drugs, especially if that person is your father or surrogate father, increases the risk of sexual abuse. Although alcohol and drugs do not cause sexual abuse, their use appears to make it easier for offenders to commit incest. Alcohol and drugs lower a person's inhibitions and are often used as an excuse to explain wrongful behaviors. Have you ever seen someone who is drinking do something that he or she would not do if sober? How did you feel watching him or her?

Rigid Families

Families with strict rules and rigidly defined sex roles are more prone to incestuous behavior than families in which rules can be bent depending on the circumstances and roles are not defined by gender. Frequently the rigid family has strict religious beliefs, and the wife and daughter have certain specific duties to the husband and father. Although sex is not among the specific duties, unquestioning obedience and service to the father usually are. Women and girls are accorded a much lower status than the males, especially the father. The father is usually much better educated than the mother and dominates the household tyranically. The mother is passive and follows the rules as carefully as the children. Children are not allowed to form outside relationships, thus limiting their access to information on how other families live and interact.

Passive/Dependent Mothers

In families where the mother is extremely dependent on her husband, the risk for sexual abuse is increased, especially if the father is predisposed toward incest. Your mother may be passive and have very little say-so over what goes on in the household. Usually she is emotionally withdrawn and shows little affection toward either her husband or you. In fact, she is child like herself, unable to fend for herself, relying on her husband totally for economic and emotional support. Generally, the passive mother gives many of her responsibilities to you. If sexual abuse does occur, your mother may believe she is unable to protect you and so accept the situation as the way things are.

Merely being a member of a large family, or having a stepparent or only one parent, or having a passive mother, or being very religious, or having a parent who is a substance abuser does not mean that you will be a victim of sexual abuse. What it does mean is that the *potential* for abuse is greater in those types of households, especially if one or both of the parents have been a victim of abuse themselves. It is important to remember that not every girl who has been sexually abused grows up to marry an abusive husband, nor does every boy who has been sexually abused become an abusive father. A single factor does not necessarily increase the risk of incest in a household. A combination of factors means that the potential for sexual abuse increases. In a situation where stress is increased, such as by the loss of a job or a spouse, the potential for some sort of abuse exists. The potential for that abuse to take the form of incest is increased in some households more than in others.

THE INCESTUOUS HOUSEHOLD

It is impossible to give a precise description of an incestuous household, but some generalizations can be made based on information gathered from reported cases. Read these generalizations, and then try the test suggested at the end of the chapter.

The incestuous household tends to be isolated, withdrawn, suspicious, and secretive. It is difficult to keep a behavior problem secret when there are a lot of people around. Adults who engage in incestuous relationships with their children tend to have trouble with relationships with other adults and thus generally have few or no friends of their own. This social isolation makes it easier for the adult to hide his abusive behavior from outsiders.

When the sexually abused child is under school age it is easy for the parent to isolate the child. When the child reaches school age, however, the opportunity for accidental disclosure increases. It is not unusual for the school-aged victim of incest to be severely restricted from outside or after-school activities. The child cannot go to the homes of other children, and other children are not allowed in the child's home. Sometimes, however, and especially if the offender is a pedophile, the child is encouraged to bring other children home. Those children may also become victims of the offender.

Abusive parents fail to see their children as persons in their own right. Instead they view their children as extensions of themselves. By ignoring the fact that the child has feelings and rights exclusively his or her own, it is easier for the parent to abuse the child without feeling guilty. This lack of empathy with the child not only allows the abuse to begin but also to continue. Finally, it makes it easier to deny the abusive behavior when it is discovered.

Role boundaries are blurred and confused in an incestuous household. The daughter who is being abused by her father is being placed in the position of a wife. The mother may become jealous of her daughter and see her as a rival instead of as a child in need of protection. At the same time that the daughter is being treated like a rival and a wife, she is also being treated as a child from whom obedience and respect are expected.

Physical boundaries are also blurred and ignored as the child's right to the privacy of his or her own body is violated. Even the child's personal space is no longer safe as the abuser demands access to the child's time in the bedroom as well as in the bathroom. This is all very confusing to the child.

Incestuous families tend to isolate themselves. Because of that they become overdependent on one another for their emotional needs and tend to fear separation. This interdependence and social isolation are increased by the secrecy that surrounds an incestuous relationship. If the secret is accidentally disclosed, the family often denies the abuse. It is not uncommon for the victim also to deny the abuse. The family then binds itself even closer together.

If the disclosure is deliberate, family members may bind themselves together to exclude the victim. They may blame the victim for disruption of the family, especially if the offender is the main economic support and is removed from the household, even though the victim would be at great risk for continued abuse if the offender were to remain.

If the victim is removed, he or she may be unable to cope with the separation and may change his or her story in order to be returned to the family. Sometimes not only the offender but other family members make the victim feel responsible for the stability of the family.

Sometimes the sexual abuse ends for no apparent reason. The offender's attentions may be shifted to another child as the victim grows older or leaves home. Sometimes the incest is discovered by a family member who is able to exert enough authority to end the abuse. No matter how the incest experience ends, the memory and the effects of it continue well into adulthood. The fact that the sexual abuse ends for the offender does not mean it ends for the victim.

Now that you have read this chapter, go back to the section entitled, "The Incestuous Household." Read it again substituting yourself for "the child." Wherever you see "the abusive adult" think about the person or people who may be abusing you. For some of you, this section did not describe an incestuous household, it described *your* family. If that is the case you need to tell a trusted and caring adult that you need help. If he or she cannot help you, continue to seek other adults until someone helps you. As you continue reading, we hope to answer even more of your questions. The next chapter identifies the various types of incest.

CHAPTER 6

Types of Incest

lthough all types of sexual abuse have an impact
upon the child, it is believed that incest between a
parent and a child is the most traumatic. There are
several reasons for that. You depend on your parents for
physical and economic support. Mothers and fathers, as
responsible parents, provide a home, food, medical care,
clothing, and many other things that you need for physical
survival.

You also depend on your parents for psychological and
emotional support. Mothers and fathers help to make their
children feel safe and protected in spite of their
vulnerability. Do you feel loved and protected in your
home?

Your parents' job is to give you guidance that will help
you become a fully functioning member of society. When a
parent engages in sexual activity with his or her child, not
only is that parent committing a crime punishable by law,
but also emotional crimes against the child. The abusive
parent is violating the child's trust and abusing the power
of his or her position in the household. The abusive parent
is denying a son or daughter the right to a normal

childhood and is disrupting the natural relationship between husband and wife as well as parent and child.

A child who is sexually abused by someone in the home has limited options, especially if other family members are made aware of the abuse and do not intervene on the child's behalf. Although some children consider running away an option, the results are frequently disastrous. Girls run away from home more often than do boys because people are more willing to help girls and provide shelter. Unfortunately, some girls are befriended by pimps who involve them in prostitution or people who are likely to continue the sexual abuse.

A child who runs away from home usually lacks skills to get a job that will pay enough to support himself or herself. Many child prostitution rings are made up of children who have run away to escape an incestuous relationship. All too often they find that they are unable to care for themselves. In addition, these children frequently have low self-esteem and lack a sense of self-worth. Drugs may be available in their new way of life and may provide a way to escape their memories. These children continue to be victimized. For a child scarred by the experience of incest, anything may seem better than what was happening at home. Have you ever thought about running away? It is a normal thought but should *not* be acted upon. Instead, talk to a trusted adult about how you feel.

You may be so starved for love that the sexual abuse is mistaken for affection. Sometimes the physical intimacy feels good. We all may have a physical response to the touch of another person whether we want to or not. Some physiological responses are automatic. If you have been deprived of a genuine parental caress, you may respond to sexual advances for lack of anything else. The thought of losing that physical closeness may prevent you from doing anything about the abusive aspects of the relationship. You may believe that the life you have is better than the unknown life you might experience if you reported the abuse. In the short run, you may be right. However, the long-term effects of incest are debilitating. You need to stop the abuse as soon as possible. When you are being sexually abused in your own home, you have no place to go. Home is where you ought to be safe, but to an incest victim home can be a frightening, hurtful place. Is your home a safe place for you to grow up and become an adult?

INCESTUOUS FATHERS

Fathers occupy a unique position in the household. Their status allows them to demand obedience, which means that sons and daughters are less likely to resist their sexual advances. Because fathers are often the main providers, other family members may be unwilling to challenge their authority. Fathers are usually larger and stronger than other members of the household, and their mere size can be an unspoken physical threat that alone may decrease the likelihood that you will resist. Finally, because fathers usually live in the household or have access to you on a regular basis, the opportunity for repeated abuse exists.

FATHER/DAUGHTER INCEST

The most commonly reported incestuous abuse is father/ daughter incest. Father/daughter incest is defined as sexual activity between a biological father, an adoptive father, a stepfather, or a surrogate father and a female child in his care.

Regardless of the blood relationship, father/daughter

incest is believed to be extremely traumatic. First and foremost, the relationship between a father and daughter is based on trust. A young girl's relationship with her father sets the stage for her later relationships with men. A father who sexually abuses his daughter is telling her that men cannot be trusted. He is telling her that affection is demonstrated by sexual behavior. He is telling her that her body is not her own, that it is property that anyone can use no matter what she thinks or wants.

Female incest victims respond to these hidden messages. Girls who have been molested by their fathers frequently display one of two types of behavior: Either they become frightened of men and show extreme reluctance to be around them, or they become promiscuous and have many sexual partners. Incest victims are often victimized later in life by other males; it is not uncommon to find that they become rape victims or marry into other abusive relationships.

Reports on father/daughter incest show that fathers, more than other male relatives involved in incestuous relationships, are more likely to go beyond fondling and engage in intercourse with their daughters. They do not seem to limit their abuse to one occasion but engage in several or many incidents of sexual abuse. Fathers appear more likely than other offenders to use physical force against their daughters.

Although incestuous behavior is usually demonstrated by some sort of sexual activity, the motivation varies. It is important to understand that a father who engages in incestuous behavior with a daughter does so for his own reasons that have nothing to do with her. Having sex with someone who does not want it or who is in a powerless position is not consensual sex. Consensual sex is sex between two equals who agree to have sex with each other.

When a person is in a position of power and uses his or her position of authority to have sex with a person who is powerless, it is considered forced sex. Forced sex is an act of aggression and hostility. Forced sex is rape, no matter who the offender is or who the victim is.

Incest does not usually happen all at once, but it can. Generally it begins slowly, with the father gently caressing you to gain your trust. Because it feels good to be caressed, you are not likely to become defensive over that behavior. It is normal for parents to caress their children and for you to enjoy being caressed. The incestuous father, however, does not stop with caressing. He advances to fondling and may go further to sexual intercourse.

Sometimes incest begins with the father engaging in exhibitionism (exposing his genitals) or voyeurism (looking at someone engaged in a private activity). The exhibitionist walks around nude more than is appropriate. He may encourage your curiosity about his genitals. If you were very young, it was not difficult for him to persuade you to touch his genitals.

The voyeur is likely to "accidentally" walk in while his daughter is changing clothes or taking a shower. Rather than immediately leaving the room, the voyeur will linger, sometimes offering to "help."

The father does not usually ask you to keep the initial behavior a secret. He waits until you have been eased into the relationship. Then when you have accepted the behavior, he tells you not to tell your mother or anyone else; it will be your "special secret." This serves three purposes. First, it implicates you in a deception that makes it more difficult for you to report the sexually abusive behavior to your mother. Second, it may give you a false sense of importance in the household and thus increase friction with other family members. Third, it appears to give you power over the father: You assume the responsibility of keeping the family together by not reporting the sexual abuse.

All of these behaviors would be warning signals to an experienced adult. But incest is not about experienced adults. It is about powerless children who are being sexually exploited.

Often a father who engages in incestuous behavior with his daughter has trouble dealing with adult relationships. In an adult/child relationship the father has no need to negotiate because he is in a position of power. In adult relationships each person has responsibilities toward the other, and both people are aware of those responsibilities. In an adult/child relationship, the adult demands and you accept. You are not aware of your rights, and you are unsure of your responsibilities beyond loving and obeying your father. Keep in mind that a father who has trouble dealing with other adults may feel good about the extra attention you give him.

The reality of an incestuous situation is that the daughter, who has been deprived of emotional support and affection, settles for the sexual relationship as the only way to be close to her father. Is the closeness between you and your father based on emotional support and affection or a sexual relationship? If you are involved in a sexual relationship, you need to reevaluate your family life.

Sarah's Story

Sarah's father always ignored her when she was a young girl. When she turned eleven she began to develop physically, and her father started to notice her. He would comment on how her clothes fit. He would tell her how nice she looked. Sarah was pleased that her father was paying attention to her. When she was younger her father never hugged her, but now he was hugging her all the time. It finally felt as if he loved her. When her father started coming into her room at night and fondling her breasts Sarah didn't like it, but she did not say anything. She was afraid that if she complained her father would return to his old ways of ignoring her.

As you can see, Sarah's father did not show her any affection until she reached puberty. The affection he did show her had nothing to do with Sarah as a person. It was more about her body.

All children desire the love and attention of their parents. Children who do not receive affection from their parents can become "starved" for attention. When that happens they often accept any attention as better than none. Although Sarah did not like the way her father showed his affection, she was afraid that if she objected he would go back to ignoring her. Sarah was vulnerable because she had been deprived of affection from her father since she was a young child. Her father took advantage of her need for love. A mature, responsible father shows affection to his children in nonsexual ways and does not use their vulnerability to take advantage of them.

A father may feel rejected by his wife and turn to his daughter for intimacy. Because she does not reject him or demand anything in return, he feels important again. A sexual relationship with you may give your father a sense of power and control that he does not feel with his wife. The reality for you may be that you feel in no position to reject your father's advances. You are obedient because you are afraid of the consequences, not because you and your father share a sense of mutual respect. Let's examine

Tamara's situation and see how the sexual abuse started and why it continued.

Tamara's Story

Tamara's stepfather was always reminding her how much he did for her, her younger sister, Katy, and their mother. "If it weren't for me, you and Katy and your mother would be on the street. I pay for the clothes on your back and the food on your plate. You would have nothing if I weren't here." Tamara did not complain when her stepfather began molesting her because she believed that if she did he would stop contributing money to the household. By the time she turned sixteen her stepfather had been having intercourse with her for three years. One day Tamara summoned up the courage to tell her stepfather to leave her alone. She said that she had applied for a job in a department store downtown and the family wouldn't need his money anymore. He laughed and told her that if she didn't do what he wanted, Katy would. Tamara did not want Katy to go through that, so she continued in the relationship with her stepfather.

Again, as in Sarah's story, Tamara's stepfather's abuse had nothing to do with her. He felt that Tamara and her mother did not show enough gratitude for his contributions to the household and that it was his right to have sex with Tamara. When Tamara felt strong enough to tell her stepfather to stop he threatened to abuse her sister. He first used her economic dependence to force her to do what he wanted. When that was insufficient he used the threat of harming her sister. Both Tamara and Katy were vulnerable.

Children do not owe adults sexual behavior in return for economic support. A man who marries a woman with children understands that he is to be a surrogate father and that it is his responsibility to help support the children. Father/daughter incest usually occurs with the oldest daughter in the house. In our society we often relegate many household and child-care duties to the oldest daughter, thus making her into a "little mother." In a home where the mother is absent or ineffective, a father who is predisposed toward incest may enlarge the role of "little mother" into that of "little wife."

Sometimes the father chooses a younger daughter because she is less aggressive than the older daughter or because the older daughter has moved away. An incestuous father may begin abusing his daughter when she is quite young. Sometimes the abuse does not begin until the daughter enters puberty and begins to develop physically. Incest can begin at any age and may continue for a long time. In order to stop it you need to get help from a caring adult.

FATHER/SON INCEST

Information on father/son incest is somewhat limited because of lack of reporting. Even in substantiated reports, fathers are reluctant to admit having sexually abused their sons. It is not uncommon for a father who has been convicted of sexually abusing a son to claim that he was so drunk at the time that he does not remember anything.

Although not all families are the same, some generalizations can be made to describe a household in which father/son incest occurs. The fathers typically fall into the same categories as those who commit father/daughter incest. That is because fathers who sexually abuse their sons are usually abusing other children in the household as well. As with father/daughter incest, in households where the son is being abused life seems to revolve around the abuser. Although some fathers who abuse their sons are homosexuals, the vast majority are not. Fathers who sexually abuse their sons are likely to be physically abusing them as well.

Alan's Story

Alan was six years old when his father first initiated sexual activity. He told Alan that he was going to teach him how men learned about sex. He cautioned Alan not to tell his mother because "women don't understand these things. This is something only men do." Alan went along because he wanted to please his father and he wanted to learn "what men do." After the first few times his father showed him some magazines with pictures of young boys having sex with older men. He asked Alan to pose for pictures. Alan objected, but his father promised to take him to Disneyland if he cooperated, so Alan let his father take pictures. Even though it made him uncomfortable, he thought it was probably all right because his father had never done anything to hurt him.

One day Alan's father took him to someone else's house where there was a boy about Alan's age. Alan watched as the boy performed oral sex on his father while the other man took pictures. Then Alan's father said he was going to take pictures of Alan having sex with the other man. Alan did not want to do that, but his father reminded him of the trip to Disneyland. On the way home Alan started to cry and said he did not want to do that anymore. His father said that was really too bad but he had no choice. He said that if Alan ever told anyone the police would take him to jail. He said that if Alan didn't obey he would show his mother the pictures of Alan having sex with the other man. Alan did not know what to do. He did not want to go to jail, and he didn't want his mother to know what had been going on. He realized that his father had tricked him, but he also felt guilty and ashamed for wanting so badly to go to Disneyland.

Alan's father was a pedophile. He very carefully led Alan into sexual activity. He never physically abused him or threatened to abuse him. At first Alan responded to his father's overtures because he did not know any better. He was curious about "what men do," and he had no reason to believe that his father would harm him. When Alan began to object, his father offered him a trip to Disneyland. Although Alan later blamed himself for wanting to go to Disneyland, the truth was that his father had bribed him.

A child does not have the reasoning capacities of an adult. A child can be tricked very easily. Adults teach children certain types of behavior by offering rewards and punishments. Alan was not at fault. His father knew that Alan wanted to go to Disneyland. He also knew that he was abusing his son and that he was engaging in criminal activity. Alan did not know that. When an adult bribes a child, the adult is well aware of what he or she is doing. The child is merely responding to the stimulus. Alan cannot be held responsible for his father's actions.

Have you ever done anything you felt uncomfortable doing in order to get something you really wanted? If so, it was a natural part of growing up. As you get older you'll begin making wiser and more responsible decisions that avoid uncomfortable situations.

Preston's Story

Preston's stepfather began sexually abusing him when Preston was ten years old. The stepfather was an alcoholic, had a violent temper, and was chronically unemployed. In order to pay the bills, Preston's mother worked as a waitress at night, leaving her husband to care for Preston and his younger sister. Instead of staying at home, Preston's stepfather usually went out as soon as his wife had left for work. He usually came home drunk and passed out before she returned. Sometimes he would wake Preston and demand that the boy fix him some food. Although his stepfather had never hit him, Preston was afraid of him because he was always yelling and cursing, and he did hit his mother. Preston always did what he asked as quickly as possible so that he could go back to bed and get away from him. The first time his stepfather asked Preston to perform oral sex on him, Preston said no and escaped into his room. His stepfather did not react until his mother came home. Then he started shouting at her and beating her. Preston woke to the fight. He did not tell his mother about his stepfather's request, but the next time his stepfather demanded the same thing Preston did as he asked.

Preston believed that his stepfather had beaten his mother because he had refused to perform oral sex. He thought he could protect her by submitting to his stepfather's demands. What would you have done in Preston's situation?

INCESTUOUS MOTHERS

Although reported cases of mother/son incest are rare, they do occur. The mother in these cases usually has no husband and is alone with her children. She uses her son as a substitute for a husband. Often she has been abused by men and feels safer and more secure in a relationship with her child. Sometimes mothers who physically abuse their children also have sexual relationships with them.

Jerry's Story

Jerry's parents were divorced when he was three years old, and his mother received custody. His father soon married again. His mother dated several men during the next three years, but none of the relationships worked out. When Jerry's father and his second wife had a baby, his mother was very bitter. She complained to Jerry about how "rotten" his father was and how men were "no good." She also started drinking a lot. Often she would come home drunk from a night out. Sometimes she would wake Jerry and tell him to come and sleep with her. Then she would fondle him and ask him to touch her breasts. Jerry did not refuse because he didn't want her to think he was "rotten" too. He was also afraid of his mother because other times when she came home she would scream at him about something he had done. Jerry never knew what to expect from his mother. He began to get bad stomachaches from stress and strain.

Jerry's mother was a dependent person, and she abused alcohol. Jerry was confused because her behavior was inconsistent. Was Jerry old enough to deal with his mother? If you were in his situation, would you have told your father? Why or why not?

Sometimes a mother engages in sexual activity with her child at the request or demand of her husband or boyfriend. She may be trying to please the husband or boyfriend and be afraid of losing him if she does not cooperate. Or she may be physically afraid of her husband or boyfriend. Not all mothers place the welfare of their children above the pleasure of another adult. Are you sure what you would do if you were being abused by your spouse?

INCEST BETWEEN BROTHERS AND SISTERS

Brother/sister incest tends to occur in families where the father is not present or is not the dominant figure. That does not mean that brother/sister incest cannot occur in other families. It can and does. Although the most commonly reported cases of incest involve father/daughter (or stepfather/daughter) relationships, it is believed that most cases of incest involve brother/sister relationships. Incest between brothers also occurs. Boys often engage in sex play with each other as part of the normal learning process.

Some sexual activity between siblings is simply a matter of normal sexual curiosity, but some is not. It is not uncommon for what starts out as curiosity to progress beyond what was expected. In cases involving a young and a much older child, the younger child may not have fully understood the nature of the "game." Sexual activity between young children and much older children usually is not a matter of simple sexual curiosity.

Sometimes the younger child is offered candy, money, or special privileges to cooperate. Or the child is intimidated by a threat of physical violence or of telling the parents about some other misbehavior. Once the child participates, a threat to tell the parents about that very participation is frequently used to gain further compliance. The older sibling may be acting to "get even" for something. He or she is very angry and takes out the anger on the younger child by degrading and humiliating him or her.

Paula's Story

Paula's brother, who was sixteen, asked her to come to his room one night, saying he had a present for her. Paula was only six years old and loved surprises. When she went into her brother's room, he said the present was under the bed. As she got down on her hands and knees to look under the bed, he exposed himself and said she had to touch his penis first. Paula pulled away from him and tried to leave the room. Her brother forced her onto the bed and told her again to touch his penis. She was very frightened but could not get away because he was holding her arm tightly. Although Paula did not tell her parents, she never went into her brother's room again.

Geoffrey's Story

Geoffrey and John were brothers. Geoffrey was seven years old and John was twelve. They shared a bedroom. One night John told Geoffrey that he was going to teach him a game that "big boys" played. He made him take off his pajamas while he did the same and then showed him how to masturbate. The next night John said they were going to play the game again, but this time he performed oral sex on Geoffrey. Geoffrey felt uncomfortable about it, but he didn't tell anyone what had happened. The next time John wanted to "play the game," Geoffrey objected. John threatened to tell their father what had been going on. Geoffrey was afraid that his father would be angry and that he would be blamed. He knew that John had a way of telling things that made them seem different from what they really were. So Geoffrey did what John wanted him to do.

Paula's brother tricked her into coming into his room, then used physical force to make her do something she did not want to do. Geoffrey's brother also tricked him, but in a different way. First John got him to "play the game." Then when Geoffrey refused to go along anymore, John threatened to tell that Geoffrey had "played the game" in the first place. John was blackmailing Geoffrey. Have you ever done something you didn't want to do because someone threatened to tell something that you already had done?

GRANDFATHER/GRANDCHILD INCEST

We tend to think of grandfathers as kindly, wise old men. Most grandfathers are that way, but some are not. Some grandfathers take advantage of the affection and respect that come with their position. We may make the mistake of thinking that because someone is old enough to be a grandparent, that person no longer has an interest in sexual activity. The reality is quite different. Older people can and do have active sex lives, and they can commit the same types of abuse that younger people commit.

Some grandfathers who sexually abuse their grand-children also abused their own children when they were younger. Sometimes a grandfather acts out his sexual fantasies with his granddaughter rather than with his own daughter. This may be because it is easier to approach a child than a woman, or because the grandfather does not view the child as a direct blood relative.

A grandfather may feel especially vulnerable to society's attitude toward aging. He may have been forced to retire, and his wife may no longer be living. Other family members may treat him as if he were less than a competent adult. All of these factors may contribute to his loss of self-esteem. He may turn to his granddaughter as one of the few people who still look up to him and respect him. He takes advantage of her trust and love for him by sexually abusing her.

Grandchildren who have been victimized by a grandparent can be just as traumatized as children who have been victimized by a parent. Their abuser is either their mother's or their father's parent. Grandparents are supposed to be affectionate with their grandchildren, and children are usually caught off guard when that affection turns to sexual abuse.

Juanita's Story

Every Saturday Juanita's grandfather took her to the racetrack. She loved horses and was fascinated by the sights and sounds. He introduced her as his "little Princess," and everyone told him how beautiful she was. Grandpa Nino seemed to know everyone at the track, and she was happy he was her grandpa.

On the way home they always stopped for ice cream and ruined their appetite for dinner. But her parents never complained, and she didn't either. This routine went on for years, and she looked forward to the weekends very much.

By the time she was twelve Juanita knew everyone at the track and cheered at each race until she was hoarse. Their rides home began to take longer, as Grandpa Nino enjoyed driving through the countryside. One day he parked the car and asked Juanita if she wanted to see Grandma's and his favorite romantic spot in the woods. Juanita agreed, and they began walking into a more heavily wooded area. It was even more beautiful than she imagined. Grandpa Nino gave her a giant bear hug and started kissing her ears and neck. When she tried to pull away, he held her even tighter and hurt her ribs. He threw her to the ground and raped her amidst the singing birds. Juanita was in shock. She began to sob and trembled uncontrollably.

Jamahl's Story

Sundays were family days, and the routine was always the same. Jamahl's grandfather got up early and cooked a huge breakfast for the family before they went to church. Jamahl knew that one day he would be standing in the pulpit just as his father was doing today and his grandfather had done in previous years. He knew he had "preacher's blood" in him, and he loved to talk in front of people. It didn't matter that he was only seven; he knew his time would come and he would be ready.

Shortly after his birthday Jamahl became an acolyte at church. He was proud of his position and performed his duties very well. After church one Saturday night he and his grandfather stayed for a while and cleaned the pews for Sunday services. When they went into the back storage room, his grandfather asked him to try on some clothing that was going to be sold at a coming church fundraiser. Jamahl liked a pair of plaid shorts, and his grandfather said he could have them on one condition. Jamahl had to massage his grandfather's penis until he ejaculated.

Jamahl knew what an erection was but had never seen anyone ejaculate. His father had told him that some things were very personal and private and that sex was one of them. But Jamahl trusted his grandfather and knew it must be okay if he asked him to do it. The shorts were an added incentive, and Jamahl masturbated his grandfather as he requested.

On the way home his grandfather told him not to tell anyone where he got the shorts or what they had been doing. Jamahl became confused and began to think that he should tell his father what happened. Was Jamahl responsible for his own behavior?

It is not uncommon for children who report sexual advances by their grandfathers to have their reports dismissed as misunderstandings because of society's unwillingness to accept that older people are sexually active. You may be told that Grandpa is senile and didn't mean what he was doing, or you may be accused of exaggerating the incident. Do you think Juanita's and Jamahl's parents would have believed them?

If you choose not to tell but instead try to avoid Grandpa, you are in a no-win situation. Although it is usually easier to avoid an abusive grandfather than an abusive parent, it is not without its complications. Your grandfather is the father of one of your parents, and he will be included in many family get-togethers. It may even be made more difficult by well-meaning parents who push you toward your grandfather saying, "Now, kiss Grandpa hello," or "Kiss Grandpa goodbye."

GRANDMOTHER/GRANDCHILD INCEST

Although little has been written or documented regarding grandmother/grandchild incest, it does occur. In today's society women outlive men, and it would not be surprising if your grandmother lived many long, productive years after your grandfather's death. Let's see what happens to Patti and Oliver in the next two scenarios.

Patti's Story

Rainy days were always a wonderful time to be at Grandma Earhart's house. She would read to Patti, and they would make chocolate chip cookies. Patti spent one weekend every two months with her grandma and enjoyed being spoiled. It was hard on Grandma since Grandpa died, but Patti tried to cheer her up with jokes she heard at school.

Patti loved to sleep in the big feather bed but was startled one morning to find Grandma Earhart in bed with her. Not a word was spoken about the incident at breakfast, and Patti just thought that her grandma was lonely or had had a bad dream. They had a wonderful day shopping, and Patti knew that all the girls would be jealous of her new outfit Monday. She would be the talk of the fifth grade.

It had been a long and tiring day, and Patti fell asleep on the sofa. Grandma Earhart half carried her upstairs and began to undress her. Patti was too tired to help put her pajamas on, so she just stood there in her underwear waiting. When Patti tried to roll over in the morning, she couldn't move. Grandma Earhart had an arm and a leg draped over her. She was also surprised to find herself nude. She struggled to get free, and her grandma woke up. "What's the matter?" Grandma Earhart asked. She started to gently stroke Patti's face and hair, and Patti began to relax. Soon she slid her hands down Patti's chest and gently kissed each breast.

Oliver's Story

Oliver was twelve years old and had been interested in girls for almost a year. He couldn't wait for his first school dance, but he was also apprehensive. He didn't know how to dance, but he imagined himself gliding across the floor with Martina in his arms. Maybe Grandma Gertie would teach him to dance.

After school on Wednesday he rode his bicycle over to Grandma Gertie's house and asked her if she would teach him to dance. Her eyes sparkled as she agreed, and Oliver was to have his first lesson on Friday. For the next eight weeks he rode to his grandmother's every Friday and learned the difference between a two-step and a polka. As the steps became more complicated, he stayed later and later. Oliver's parents were pleased that he showed such an interest in dancing and encouraged him to spend the night so he could practice longer. His seventh-grade dance was less than three months away, and he wanted to be ready and confident.

Oliver enjoyed the time alone with his grandmother. They would pop popcorn and eat it in between stories of all her dates and boyfriends. Grandma Gertie had always been special in his heart, and now he loved her even more. He wanted to ask her how he would know whether or not he should kiss a girl, but he hesitated. When she left the room for a minute he got up his courage.

Grandma Gertie told Oliver that it was very difficult to figure out what a girl wanted him to do, but that she could probably show him how a girl would act. With that, she dimmed the lights and turned the music on. As they danced Oliver noticed that she slid her hands up and down his back and over his buttocks. He didn't remember that happening in previous lessons, but it felt kind of nice. She had taught him to hold the girl about fourteen inches away from his body, but now she pressed her body close to his. He could feel his body beginning to respond, and then Grandma Gertie kissed him hard on the mouth. As he took a step backward, she took a step forward and kissed him again. When the music stopped he could feel his heart pounding.

In both instances Patti and Oliver were victims of sexual abuse. They felt safe with their grandmothers and were subtly manipulated into a situation that was sexually satisfying for their grandmothers. Neither Patti nor Oliver did anything wrong. As you can see, force and violence do not have to take place for you to be sexually abused. Notice the difference in age and power between the grandmothers and the grandchildren. Although this type of incest is rare, it still happens.

UNCLE/NIECE INCEST

The relationship between uncles and nieces is generally quite different from that of a child and a parent or a child and a grandparent. Usually an uncle does not live in the same household as his niece. You are not usually dependent upon your uncle for financial support. Nevertheless, uncle/niece incest is not uncommon. Uncles are trusted members of the family and so have access to you even though they do not live in the same house. After stepfathers and grandfathers, uncles are the third most often reported sexual abusers of relatives.

Cecilia Ann's Story

Despite the family's comments about how much they disliked Christian, Cecilia Ann thought he was exciting to be with. She never knew what he would say or do, and she found that refreshing. The rest of her relatives were boring. Although she was only seven years old, she felt that she was a fairly good judge of character, and Uncle Christian was all right in her book.

The Fourth of July was coming, and her parents asked if she would mind spending a three-day weekend with Uncle Christian. They had a family wedding to attend in Oregon and thought she would prefer to stay at home and play with her friends. Cecilia Ann was elated and couldn't wait to call her best friend Marsha with the news. She was also hoping that Marsha would be able to spend the night with her on the Fourth so they could stay up late and watch the fireworks.

On Thursday afternoon she went with Uncle Christian to see her parents off at the airport. On the way home they stopped at the best pizza parlor in town but ate only half of their pizza; they needed to save room for the popcorn and ice cream that he promised for later. He asked if she wanted to rent a couple of videos for the evening, and she squealed with delight. At the video store she picked out two movies and Uncle Christian slipped into the back room and found a couple for himself.

Cecilia Ann put "Mary Poppins" into the VCR, and Uncle Christian motioned for her to sit next to him on the sofa. She snuggled into his side, and he put his arm around her. Periodically she got up to sing and dance around the room. Uncle Christian laughed, and then he got up and danced with her. She enjoyed having him bow to her and twirl her under his arms across the room. Soon he made popcorn, and then he slowly began to massage her neck and shoulders. If only her parents could see them now they would take back all the mean things they had said about Uncle Christian.

After they had rewound the "Mary Poppins" tape, Uncle Christian said it was only fair that he get to watch one of his movies. Cecilia Ann agreed, and she sat there motionless trying to figure out what the movie was all about. She saw children playing together and wondered what game they were playing. Soon an adult entered the scene and left with one of the children. The next thing Cecilia Ann saw made her feel uncomfortable. The man began undressing the little girl and touching her private parts. Uncle Christian pulled her closer and kissed the top of her head. The girl in the movie seemed to be enjoying it, but why did Cecilia Ann feel so uncomfortable? She jumped up and turned off the television. Uncle Christian asked if she wanted to play that game, and she said, "No!" He said that he had spent a lot of money on her and they were going to play that game, no matter what she said.

The next three days were the longest days of Cecilia Ann's life. Was this what her family meant by not liking Uncle Christian? If they had known this was how he would behave, why had they let him take care of her? What had she done to deserve such a horrible punishment? She promised herself to be a good girl when her parents returned. In the meantime she withdrew into herself to survive the ordeal. Even Marsha never came to her rescue.

Do you think Cecilia Ann's parents knew that Uncle Christian would sexually abuse her? Probably not! They might have disliked him for a variety of reasons, such as smoking too much, overeating or drinking, or swearing around children. Cecilia Ann was not being punished by her parents. They trusted Christian, and Cecilia Ann enjoyed being with him. Her parents thought they were doing what was in Cecilia Ann's best interests.

Could Marsha have rescued Cecilia Ann? Only if she had caught them engaging in some type of sexual activity and gone home to tell her parents. But do you think Marsha's parents would have believed her? If they had a good relationship, yes! Keep in mind that if you tell the truth all the time, people are more apt to believe you when the truth is hard to believe or accept.

OTHER FORMS OF INCEST

You may also be sexually abused by cousins, brothers-in-law, and more distant relatives. You may be victimized by more than one relative. You may be victimized by family members and others outside the family. The variations of sexual abuse of children by family members are many. But no matter what the relationship is, some things are always the same. Let's review the commonalities again.

It is a crime for a person with power, either because of his or her size, strength, authority, or position in the household, to sexually abuse a child who cannot fight back because of his or her lack of power. Your lack of power may stem from being smaller, or from economic dependence, or from fear of physical abuse or other threats. In some cases your lack of power may simply stem from the fact that you love the abuser and do not want to displease him or her.

Another commonality is that the abuser is betraying your trust because you have no reason to be suspicious. The abuser is violating your right to the privacy of your own body and personal space. But most of all, the abuser is violating your right to a "normal" childhood. The abuser is creating an emotional trauma that may affect you for the rest of your life. Sexual abuse within a family is the exception to the rule; it does not occur in healthy families.

So far, most of this book has dealt with girls rather than boys as victims. Although there are many similarities, there are also some differences. Therefore, Chapter 7 examines boys as victims.

Boys as Victims

The statistics on sexually abused boys are even less informative than those for sexually abused girls. It is believed that of the 12 to 33 percent of sexually abused boys, anywhere from 6 to 50 percent of them are abused by parents or stepparents.

Boys are less likely to report sexual abuse than are girls. Whereas girls are socialized to be passive, which makes them more vulnerable to various kinds of victimization, boys are socialized to be aggressive, self-reliant, and independent. Boys who are not physically aggressive or self-assertive or who appear to be weak are labeled "sissies" and "nerds" by their peers. Girls are not expected to be sexually active, so the shame that can accompany sexual abuse often keeps them quiet. Boys are expected to be sexually active, so reporting sexual abuse sometimes is taken as a joke. These social attitudes help create an atmosphere that makes it difficult for a boy to tell someone when he is a victim of incest.

It is important to remember that boys are children also and are in very much the same situation as are girls. Boys also need love and nurturing and guidance. They are dependent on their parents for financial and emotional support. Boys are also told to be obedient and to respect their parents. Society may expect different things from boys outside the household, but at home boys still occupy a position of dependence and are expected to show the same deference to their parents as are girls.

Still, society's attitude toward sexually abused boys makes it even harder for them to report the abuse. Rod McKuen, a popular poet of the 1970s, was sexually abused by his stepaunt and stepuncle when he was seven years old. He never told anyone about it until forty-four years later when he was speaking before the National Committee for the Prevention of Child Abuse. Can you imagine keeping a secret of that magnitude for forty-four years? Why do you think he remained silent for so long? There are numerous reasons for silence, but Rod McKuen felt humiliated. As we identify the most common reasons for boys not reporting abuse, you may see yourself or a close friend in a similar situation. Remember, boys *are* sexually abused and you are *not* alone. Let's see how Chad was abused and humiliated and why he felt he couldn't tell anyone.

Chad's Story

Junior high school was supposed to be fun, but all Chad saw when he walked into his new school was graffiti on the walls and groups of guys hanging out in the hallways. He had been nervous at breakfast even before his parents warned him not to get involved with any of the gangs. Chad had never had trouble making friends, so he was unprepared for what happened at his locker when three guys approached him.

"Hey, pretty boy," said one of the guys wearing a red

bandanna. "Are you a narc?" Chad started to turn around and answer him, but the guy called Sly shoved him hard against the lockers. Then the three boys walked away and Chad heard them saying that next time they would show the "pretty boy" just who really ran the school.

As the months passed Chad began to make new friends and to adjust to the freedom between classes. There was just enough time to visit briefly with friends or to use the restroom. His parents were both pleased with their new jobs, especially his mother. Her promotion was the reason behind their move in the first place. Overall, life was beginning to settle down into a fairly normal routine for all of them.

Chad was beginning to feel some pressure from the two gangs in the school. Sly's gang, called the Blood Brothers, had a few interesting guys in it, but no one could tell Chad what bonded them all so closely together. The other gang, the Castaways, seemed not to care about getting an education and hung out on street corners almost every night. Chad simply preferred being friends with everyone he liked, and he avoided those people who made him feel uncomfortable.

The school year was rapidly ending, and Chad couldn't wait for summer vacation. He was daydreaming and didn't notice Sly, Miguel, Blake, and Eric enter the restroom together and lock the door. Before Chad knew it, he was lying face down on the floor with his pants half off. Three guys were holding him down while Sly sodomized him. "Now you know why we're called the Blood Brothers," laughed Sly. "You've just been initiated into our gang. Whether or not you want to be a member, you are!" Chad finally went limp, and they released him when another gang member pounded on the door and said someone was coming.

He barely had his jeans pulled up when Mr. Ravenel walked in. "What's going on here, Chad? Is everything all right?" Blake said that Chad wasn't feeling well and that they had followed him into the restroom in case he needed some help. Mr. Ravenel looked at Chad and said that he did look flushed and sweaty. Then he turned to Miguel and Eric and said, "You know, I misjudged you two boys. It was very thoughtful of you to come to Chad's assistance." With that, Mr. Ravenel left the room.

How would you have felt if you were Chad? Would you have been able to go home and tell your parents what had happened? Why, or why not? In this situation Chad was humiliated and powerless. Even Mr. Ravenel was fooled into believing that he had been sick and the other boys were helping him.

It is crucial for Chad to tell an adult whom he trusts. How many other students have been "initiated" by the Blood Brothers at Harper Junior High? If someone had reported the sexual abuse before Chad entered the school he might not have been sexually abused. Although Chad may feel humiliated, he did nothing wrong and could not have prevented the abuse. He can, however, stop future assaults.

You may be afraid to report sexual abuse out of fear of being ridiculed for not being able to protect yourself. Others may call you "sissy" even though you were overpowered. No one really expects a young boy to protect himself against an older or bigger and stronger adult, especially if that adult is a close family member. Most boys, and most men for that matter, are not Rambo or Bruce

Lee. T. E. Lawrence, an English soldier known as Lawrence of Arabia, was sexually abused while he was imprisoned. He was unable to defend himself because he was powerless and in a position of dependence. When people think of Lawrence of Arabia, they do not think of a "sissy." He was abused not because he was weak or cowardly but because his captors abused their power over him.

As a son, brother, grandson, or nephew, you do not expect to be placed in a situation where you have to physically defend your body from assault by a trusted family member. However, family members can be the assailants, and the abuse often occurs in the least expected situation. Just see what happens to Arthur.

Arthur's Story

Donald and Arthur are fifteen and eight years old, respectively. They have never been very close as brothers, but with time they have begun to tolerate each other a little bit more. As a member of the wrestling team, Donald was always working out with weights to keep in shape. The garage had been converted into a free weight room, and Arthur was fascinated with all the barbells. Donald hated it when Arthur watched him work out, but his father said that Arthur had a right to be in the garage.

The sectional wrestling meet was only two weeks away, and Donald spent all his free time in the garage. As he entered one morning for a workout, he saw Arthur lying on his back pretending to lift a heavy barbell. Donald walked over and picked up a 150-pound barbell. He told Arthur that he would help him lift it correctly and then they could work out together. Arthur was elated and listened intently to his brother's instructions. Donald told him he could get hurt or become pinned if he didn't have a spotter when he used a barbell such as the one he held.

Donald talked on and on about repetitions and sets and didn't notice that his brother was getting impatient. "Come on," Arthur said. "Let's stop talking and start pumping some iron." While Arthur positioned himself on his back, Donald picked up the barbell and held it over him. Arthur put his hands on the bar, and they began doing repetitions together. Donald held most of the weight, but Arthur began to tire after the eleventh repetition. All of a sudden Donald let the barbell down onto Arthur's chest and wouldn't pick it up. Arthur was pinned under the barbell. The more he struggled, the heavier the weight felt. "You little bastard. You've always been a pain in the ass and now I'm going to fix you," said Donald. With that, he took his shorts off and stood over Arthur. He forced his younger brother to perform oral sex on him before he would lift the barbell. The hatred in Donald's eyes convinced Arthur that he could never be alone with his brother again. But what would happen the next time his parents left him in Donald's care? Arthur ran outside and threw up in the bushes. What was he going to do?

Do you think Donald sexually abused his brother because Arthur watched him work out in the garage? Of course not! Being watched working out does not normally lead a person to such a violent act. There was obviously some deep-rooted resentment in Donald that Arthur was not aware of. Your assailant may not give you any warning signs before you are assaulted. Remember, the fact that there is a large difference between you and your siblings does *not* mean that you are the potential victim of sexual assault by a brother or a sister. It does mean, however, that even brothers and sisters sexually abuse one another.

A boy may not report sexual abuse because he thinks no one will believe him. Most of the news reports about incest involve girls, so it seems that boys are seldom victimized. Experts believe that sexual abuse of boys is significantly underreported, that for every two girls who are sexually abused, one boy is abused. Some experts believe that the ratio may be one to one. Again, denial makes reporting more difficult. Fathers are more willing to admit their victimization of female children than male children because father/son incest is seen as violating a double taboo—sex with a family member and homosexuality.

Dmitri's Story

As the eldest child of older parents, Dmitri was petrified by his father's mere presence. The father ruled the family with an iron hand, and all of them knew better than to question or challenge anything he said. Dmitri can't even remember a time when he was not being sexually abused by his father. Mr. Shistakovich worked long and hard hours in the coal mine and made a decent wage. The neighbors considered him a God-fearing family man who kept to himself and took care of his house.

Dmitri had already begun his growth spurt although he was only twelve. He knew that he was becoming a man, and his health education class at school had prepared him well. In class they also talked about being a man in terms of marrying and having children. Dmitri knew that he would be a better father than his own father was to him, but he still loved his father very much.

Ms. Hallman, the health teacher, always made them answer "what if" questions. The one that he kept hearing over and over in his mind was, "Would you report sexual abuse at home if you knew your name and the charges would be in tomorrow's newspaper for all of your friends to read?" The class all voted anonymously that they would, but Dmitri knew he lied. How could he report the abuse at home? No one would believe him. Even more important, would he have any friends left? Would they all think he was a homosexual? He couldn't wait to start dating girls, but who would go out with him once they saw the charges against his father? His mother never complained about his father and was devoted to him. Would she believe that her husband of eighteen years was homosexual?

Dmitri has only the wisdom of a twelve-year-old, and so it is easy for him to make mistakes in his thinking. Although he has learned about sexual abuse in his health education class, he still has important misunderstandings that prevent him from reporting his own abuse. First, the major issues in any sexual assault are power and dominance, not sex. Mr. Shistakovich's satisfaction came from overpowering Dmitri, not sexual pleasure.

Second, Mr. Shistakovich's background may have taught him to be aggressive and competitive and to view physical force as a natural and healthy way to express himself. It does not mean that he is homosexual. Although some fathers who abuse their sons are considered latent homosexuals, statistics indicate that fathers who sexually abuse their sons are overwhelmingly heterosexual. The same is true of other male family members who abuse boys in their care. It is not unusual for a father who sexually abuses his son also to abuse alcohol.

And last, the sexual relationship with his wife does not determine whether or not Mr. Shistakovich will sexually abuse his children. Even today in some cultures, children are considered property and parents can do what they wish with them. Fortunately for you, children in the United States are protected by laws that recognize your uniqueness and rights. Dmitri needs to talk with Ms. Hallman as soon as possible regarding the abuse that is occurring at home. Boys are victims and need to speak up about their experiences for the sake of all of the other male victims who are walking around in deafening silence.

Physical abuse often coexists with sexual abuse. Boys are more likely than girls to be physically threatened or to fear physical abuse. Therefore, a boy may be afraid to report the abuse because he has been physically threatened by the abuser. Statistics indicate that violence is more often used against boys who are sexually abused than girls. Again, that seems to be a result of the social conditioning that teaches girls to be passive and boys to be aggressive. The reality is that it is no easier for a boy to defend himself physically against the advances of an older, bigger, and stronger adult than it is for a girl.

Kyunghi's Story

Captain Pham of the Los Angeles Police Department was one of the most feared policemen the force had ever hired. He received numerous honors, citations, and awards from the department and the city, but everyone knew he bent the law when it came to catching criminals. When Kyunghi was younger he had loved riding in his father's patrol car. He enjoyed the high-speed chases and flashing lights and listening to the codes on the radio. He did not enjoy, however, seeing his father handcuff and beat suspected criminals. More than once his father had beaten a man unconscious and said that the man was resisting arrest. Although Kyunghi was not supposed to ride in the police car when his father was on duty, his father sometimes forced him to. Captain Pham wanted him to learn what life was like on the streets. These lessons in life also taught Kyunghi to fear his father and fear for his own safety.

Kyunghi tried not to make his father angry, and he obeyed him without question. Unfortunately, this allowed his father to sexually abuse him. At first his father said he would show Kyunghi how to be a policeman, and he handcuffed him and laughed while Kyunghi struggled to get loose. No one knew that Captain Pham later forced Kyunghi to have anal sex with him. At age six Kyunghi became the victim of his father's incestuous behavior.

Rather than handcuffing Kyunghi all the time, his father laid his police revolver on the pillow and warned that he would "blow his brains out" if Kyunghi resisted or made any noise. For years the boy passively submitted to his father.

To cope with the sexual abuse, Kyunghi learned to dissociate. Although his body was being violated by his father, his mind and thoughts were elsewhere. His mind always took him to a place where he was safe from all harm. There Kyunghi spent hundreds of hours fantasizing about killing his father with the police revolver. Would he be considered a criminal and tried for murder, or could he convince a jury that it was self-defense?

*　　*　　*

What would you have done in Kyunghi's situation? Would you have tried to resist Captain Pham's incestuous behavior? If so, what would you have done? Be specific with your answer. Did Kyunghi have reason to believe that his father would kill him if he didn't submit? In this instance Kyunghi did the right thing. He had to submit to live. However, he also needed to report the sexual abuse to a trusted adult. He might even have been able to contact one of his father's past police partners and get support from him.

Most boys who report sexual abuse, however, seem to wait until they have become adolescents. Can you guess why? They wait because they feel more secure about being able to defend themselves when they are older. Would you have reported the sexual abuse at age nine or would you have waited until you were older?

As you can see, these are very difficult questions for boys to face. On one hand society tells you that you should be able to defend yourself physically. But at the same time boys are still children who need to be protected from sexual abusers. Mixed messages make it very difficult for boys when they are trying to decide whether or not they should report sexual abuse. You always need to report sexual abuse so it can be stopped.

Homosexuality is defined as an attraction to persons of the same sex. Often a boy who has been sexually abused by his father or another male relative does not report the abuse for fear of being labeled a homosexual. A sexually abused boy does not choose who will abuse him, just as a sexually abused girl does not choose who will abuse her. In both cases the choice is that of the abuser. Your sexual orientation does *not* depend on other people's actions.

Let's examine Lee's situation and see how he interprets the actions of his Uncle Blair.

Lee's Story

Lee was artistically talented and very good-looking. As a freshman he was only fourteen and a bit shy. He had no interest in girls yet, but he loved to work with the drama club putting on plays and musicals. His friends talked about sex all the time and whom they would love to be involved with. Michael had a crush on Cindy. Gunther had already been to the movies with Ursula, and Lee still had no interest in dating. He constantly asked himself what was wrong, and he always came to the same conclusion—he must be gay.

Lee knew he had to be gay because his Uncle Blair had started sexually abusing him when he was only seven years old. He had overheard his family talking about Uncle Blair as a "confirmed bachelor" and had assumed that that was the way adults referred to a gay family member. Why else would Uncle Blair force him to have oral sex? Lee had tried to ask his two older brothers if Uncle Blair had ever forced them to have oral sex, but he couldn't get the words out. Besides, if he weren't gay, why wasn't he interested in girls the way all his friends were?

Uncle Blair didn't look gay, but Lee didn't know what a gay person was supposed to look like. Wasn't Rock Hudson gay and no one knew it? Uncle Blair was tall, tanned, and had huge muscles from working out at the fitness center. Why did he sexually abuse Lee for years? Did he pick on Lee because he was the youngest and smallest of the three boys or because he was the only one with blond hair? All Lee knew was that he didn't willingly engage in oral sex. In fact, just before the abuse ended he had told Uncle Blair that he would bite his penis if he forced him to do it one more time. Lee was only ten when he told his uncle that, but he never forgot those years of sexual abuse and always wondered why his uncle had picked on him. He was convinced that the years of sexual abuse by a man now meant that he was a homosexual and would never be interested in girls.

The age at which you begin dating and developing an interest in the opposite sex is related to your maturity level and readiness. Lee's lack of interest in girls at age fourteen is absolutely normal. His sexual orientation is not determined by his uncle's actions. Incest victims are often selected by age, physical attributes, and powerlessness; thus Lee was the perfect victim for his Uncle Blair. If you are questioning your sexual orientation because of sexual abuse, you need to see a school counselor or a therapist who can help you deal with your feelings. When you are ready to date and become involved with girls, you will. Until that time, however, you should continue developing your special talents.

If a boy has been abused by his mother he may not report the abuse for fear of being labeled mentally ill for having sex with her. In our society it is considered more acceptable for an older man to have sex with a young female than for an older woman to have sex with a young male. Our society does not seem willing to accept that some mothers do molest their children. Whereas most people would react negatively to the thought of a father giving his daughter a bath when she is quite capable of bathing herself, the thought of a mother bathing an equally capable son does not arouse much suspicion. After all, mothers are supposed to touch their children. But when does that touching become incestuous behavior? Notice how Wally feels uncomfortable and trapped by his mother.

Wally's Story

Unlike most of his junior high classmates, Wally knew what he wanted to do with his life. Joe Montana had been his idol for years, and Wally wanted to be a professional football player. To follow in Joe Montana's footsteps, he had to become the best quarterback his conference had ever seen. Mr. Washington spent hours with his son practicing how to throw the perfect spiral. He even hung a tire from the old oak tree so Wally could practice throwing through a moving target. His younger sister Letty was a cheerleader, and she loved to brag about her "big brother" the quarterback.

Everyone in the family was supportive of Wally's dream. After every peewee football game his whole family would greet him with words of encouragement and lots of hugs. His teammates' parents would wait until the coach was done with his comments, but Wally's mom would always throw her arms around his neck and begin kissing him in front of the team. Although he was embarrassed by her overaffectionate behavior, he was happy that his family cared so much about him. His teammates teased him about his mom's behavior, but they also told him how lucky he was to have such a loving family.

Once home, Wally would take a long, hot shower. His mom would apply liniment to any sore areas and rub all his aches and pains away. She would make him laugh by kissing his neck and nibbling on his ears. She always managed to raise his spirits if the team lost. While she was performing her ritual, Mr. Washington would run the tape and critique each play, offering his personal advice. He taped every game that Wally played in, both home and away. It was truly a family affair.

Wally practiced every day in the summer and began throwing to his favorite receiver, Derrick. They knew each other's moves forward and backward. Scouts from opposing teams said they were an "invincible duo." His family never missed a game, and the after-game rituals continued. But Wally began to sense that something was changing although he couldn't put his finger on it.

After one particularly rough game when he was sacked four times, his mom pulled back the shower curtain and began to wash his back and buttocks. Before he knew it she had spun him around and was also washing his chest and genitals. Just as quickly she left the bathroom and waited for him in his bedroom. Although his mom had been waiting for him in his bedroom for years, he now felt awkward and uncomfortable. But he shrugged it off and decided those sacks had jarred something loose in his brain.

As usual, his mom began rubbing liniment into his sore neck and shoulders. Although the warmth felt good, he thought his mom was caressing him rather than massaging him. Soon her kisses on the neck became kisses on the lips. Mrs. Washington told him how proud of him she was as she began to fondle his genitals. Wally prayed that his father would rescue him but knew that he was busy watching the tape and would be preoccupied for an hour.

As the football season progressed Wally's performance on the field began to deteriorate. All he could think about in the huddle was his mom kissing him and fondling his genitals. He tried to lock the bathroom door, but his mom had had the lock removed so that his younger cousins couldn't get locked in. Whenever they were alone in the house she would sneak up behind him and begin kissing him or grab his butt. One night when his father was out of town on business, he woke up to find his mom caressing his penis. At that moment Wally vowed he would never play football again. Maybe then he could escape his mom's incestuous behavior.

When did Mrs. Washington's behavior change from being overaffectionate to sexually abusive? Do you think Wally's father would have believed him if he had described his mom's sexual abuse? Could Wally have changed the after-game ritual to minimize his vulnerability? If so, how? As you can see, even families that appear to be loving and supportive can hide sexual abuse.

Wally was not mentally ill and did not willingly engage in sexual contact with his mom. He was powerless, and his mother knew how to manipulate the situation. It would be very difficult for Mr. Washington to believe that his wife was sexually abusing their son. Mrs. Washington had been very careful to display only appropriate behavior when other people were around. That does *not* mean that she did not sexually abuse Wally. It means that she calculated every move very carefully, and Wally may have to tell several adults before someone believes him.

Some people are overaffectionate by nature. That does not mean that they are prone to be sexual abusers. It does mean, however, that where, when, and how someone touches you determines whether or not it is sexual abuse. You are the only person who can give someone else permission to touch your body.

*   *   *

Another reason for not wanting to report an incestuous relationship with a mother is that a boy may be strongly attached to her. Mother/son incest usually occurs in a household where no father figure is present. Observe how Tyler feels when his father is sent to prison and his mother turns to him for sexual intimacy.

Tyler's Story

Tyler's father often beat his mother in front of him. Tyler would try to defend her, but he was only ten years old and much smaller than his father. After one particularly bad beating the police came. Tyler's father was arrested and eventually sent to prison for assault. Both Tyler and his mother were relieved to have him out of the house. Tyler loved his mother very much, and it hurt him to see her abused. He felt protective of her and was happy that they could finally be together without being afraid of his father.

Shortly after his father had been removed from the house, Tyler began sleeping in his mother's bed. At first they only cuddled with each other. One night Tyler's mother put her hand inside his pajama bottoms and began fondling his penis. Because Tyler loved her he did not object, but when he thought about it the next day he was upset and confused. He did not know what to do. He did not want to hurt his mother, and besides he felt partly responsible because while she had been touching him he had had an erection.

It is very difficult for a child to watch one parent physically abuse the other parent. How would you feel if your father beat your mother? Would you feel differently if your mother beat your father? Why, or why not? Would you feel relieved or guilty if the abusive parent were eventually sent to jail? Would you be angry at the judicial system if the abusive parent were never punished? Why?

Tyler is trying to deal with several feelings at the same time. First, it is hard for him to accept his inability to protect his mother from his father's beatings. Mr. Vanhorn is simply bigger and stronger than Tyler, and there is nothing he can do about it. An adult male can always overpower a ten-year-old boy.

Second, Tyler is both relieved and sad that his father is going to prison. He is relieved because he wanted the beatings to stop and he knew of no other way than police involvement. He is sad because he doesn't want the family broken up. At times his father can be warm and caring.

Last but probably most difficult to deal with are his mother's sexual advances. Was Tyler now the little "man of the house"? Did his mother have the right to expect sexual intimacy from her son? The answer to both questions is no! Tyler did not consent to the sexual advances just because he had an erection. Researchers have proven repeatedly that male infants have erections. Erections are often responses to physical stimuli, and they cannot always be controlled. Tyler did not initiate the sexual abuse by sleeping in a bed with his mother. Many children have slept in a bed with a parent for security reasons after the parents have separated. Parents do not normally sexually abuse their children. Rather, they try to protect them and make them feel safe. If you were Tyler, would you have felt safe with his mother before she fondled his penis? Most boys would have felt comforted and secure after a parent was sent to jail for physical abuse. Unfortunately, Mrs. Vanhorn displayed inappropriate sexual behavior with Tyler, which made him feel confused and upset. Remember, though, that Tyler behaved as any normal boy would have.

Mother/son incest has been thought to be less traumatic than sexual abuse by a male. However, interviews with men imprisoned for rape have revealed that the men were sexually abused by their mothers when they were children. It is also well documented that many men who sexually abuse their own children were themselves abused as children.

If a boy has been abused by his mother or another female relative, he may fail to report it for fear of being seen as abnormal, because boys are supposed to "enjoy" sex. If he complains, he may think, people may question his masculinity. After reading Floyd's story, do you question his masculinity? Why, or why not?

Floyd's Story

Floyd's Aunt Elaine came to live with the family when he was seven years old. She often took care of him while his parents were out. Floyd enjoyed being with his aunt because she didn't treat him like a baby. She took him places and played games with him. One evening she introduced Floyd to a new game. She explained that it was a game all boys and girls played. She also told him not to tell his parents because they thought he was still a baby and wouldn't let him play. Aunt Elaine then rubbed Floyd's penis and showed him how to rub her labia.

The first few times Floyd found the game interesting, but after a while he got tired of it, especially when it was the only game she wanted to play any more. When Floyd refused to cooperate, Aunt Elaine asked what was wrong with him. She said that if a boy weren't interested in sex he must be "abnormal." She told him that if he didn't play she would tell his friends and his parents. Floyd didn't want his friends to think that he was weird and he didn't want his parents to know what had been going on, so he continued to play the game with his aunt until she moved into her own apartment.

At seven years of age Floyd had no idea what was expected of boys and sex. He did know that he didn't want to be labeled "abnormal." Floyd also had an erection when his aunt touched his penis. Notice the similar physiological response when Floyd and Tyler had their penises stroked. This is perfectly normal in boys. Why was Floyd also afraid that his parents would blame him if they found out?

Although all incestuous households are dysfunctional, families where boys are abused seem to be even more chaotic. In a household where a boy is being abused by his father or stepfather, other children in the family are usually being abused as well. In almost half of the families where the father or surrogate father was reported as sexually abusing his son, other children were also being victimized.

THE EFFECT OF INCEST ON BOYS

Boys who have been sexually abused by their fathers or other male family members react in different ways, but some general behaviors occur. The most common re-action is *homophobia*, defined as an irrational fear of homosexuality. A boy who has been sexually abused by a male may spend a lot of time trying to convince his peers that he is not gay. He may do so by taunting other children he perceives as weak and therefore "feminine." He may physically abuse smaller children in an attempt to demonstrate his "masculinity." He may frequently initiate conversations about his desire to have sex with girls. A boy who has been sexually victimized by another family member may become physically aggressive toward others, especially persons more vulnerable than he is. Boys are socialized to be aggressive and to control their environment. Therefore, a boy who has been sexually abused may tend to compensate for his feelings of powerlessness by becoming overaggressive and domineering. Unfortunately, this type of behavior can evolve into exactly the sort of abusive action that caused the boy to be overaggressive in the first place. A boy who has been sexually abused needs to be reassured that the abuse was not his fault but a misuse of power. It was easy for the abuser to victimize him because he was smaller, younger, dependent, and vulnerable.

Male victims of incest may have difficulty forming relationships with their peers. Sometimes they feel more comfortable with much younger children. Younger children are less threatening and can be more easily dominated than someone of the same age. Notice how Billy's homophobic fears cause him to behave inappropriately and lose his friends. As you read Billy's story, try to put yourself in his situation. Can you understand his fears and frustration?

Billy's Story

Billy was ten years old when his father began sexually abusing him. It had started as a game with his father showing him how to masturbate. By the time Billy was twelve his father was forcing him to perform oral sex. One day his mother caught his father abusing him. She told her husband to leave Billy alone, but she did not report the abuse. Although Billy's father did not bother him again, Billy was convinced that his friends would somehow "know" that his father had been having sex with him. Billy knew that men who had sex with other men were homosexuals. He also knew that his friends made fun of homosexuals and called them names like "faggot" and "queer" and "sissy." Billy thought that because his father had had sex with him he was a homosexual.

Even though there was no way his friends could know that he had been sexually abused, Billy was determined to prove that he was not a sissy. When with his friends he was always the first one to call someone else a name. He mostly picked on the smaller kids. One day at school Billy saw a younger boy trip and fall. Instead of helping the boy up, Billy began to make fun of him and call him a sissy. The boy picked himself up and said to Billy, "I'm not a sissy. You are." Billy ran up to the boy and started punching him. One of the teachers saw the fight and sent Billy to the principal's office. Billy was suspended for three days. When he came back to school his friends stayed away from him and started calling him "Billy the Bully."

The little boy who called Billy a sissy had no way of knowing that Billy had been sexually abused by his father. Billy did not understand that his sexual orientation is not a result of child abuse. Unfortunately, he had not received any counseling after his abuse was discovered, so he had no way of knowing that he was not a homosexual. All he knew was that he and his friends made fun of homosexuals and he did not want his friends to make fun of him. The end result was that Billy became homophobic.

In trying to prove that he was not homosexual, Billy not only beat up a child younger and smaller than himself, he also alienated his friends and got suspended from school. How would you feel if you had a friend who was always quick to call names or to point out a weakness? Would you feel comfortable with such a friend? If Billy's parents had obtained counseling for him (and themselves), Billy could have had the opportunity to express his fears about homosexuality. The counselor could have explained the difference between a sexually abusive experience and sexual orientation. The counselor could also have helped Billy deal with his emotions such as anger at being abused and the shame he may have felt at being unable to protect himself. The counselor would have helped Billy recognize that he was not at fault and that there was nothing he could have done. Billy would have learned that his father was responsible for the abuse, not he. The counselor could also have helped Billy direct his anger more appropriately.

Billy's fears concerning his sexuality would have increased if he had spent a lot of time discussing how he wanted to have sex with girls. The girls in his age group would eventually have heard him talk and would probably have stayed away from him. Without counseling, Billy could easily have decided that they rejected him because he was homosexual, whereas the real reason would have been because he made them nervous. Billy would have reacted to the perceived rejection by becoming even angrier and more aggressive. Again, a counselor could have put things back into proper perspective and helped Billy learn to interact more appropriately.

Even though Billy had been the victim of his father's abuse, he developed problems that extended beyond his life at home. His family had done nothing to help him come to terms with what had happened. While it was good that the abuse stopped, that was insufficient to help Billy. He needed to talk about what had happened with someone he could trust.

Boys who have been victims of incest may have difficulty in forming intimate relationships. Some adult victims of incest become sexually promiscuous in an attempt to assert their masculinity. Others avoid sexual relationships altogether. Because of the lack of reporting of sexual crimes against boys, victims may view themselves as "freaks." This situation is made worse by the socialization of boys, which teaches them to control their emotions, so that they are unable to talk about their experiences. Many times male victims of sexual abuse have parenting problems specifically related to their own abuse. They may become so fearful of sexually abusing their own children that they avoid any kind of intimacy with them.

It is important to remember that just because you have been sexually abused by a family member does not mean that you will sexually abuse your own children. Counseling has been very helpful to men who have had those fears. A good counselor can help you understand that what happened was not your fault and help direct your feelings of powerlessness and anger into constructive channels that will not be harmful to you or to others.

Sometimes boys who have been sexually victimized by relatives experience changes in their physical habits. You may begin wetting the bed at night. Or you may find yourself becoming sexually stimulated at inappropriate times. These physical side effects can add to the humiliation that you feel. If these things are happening to you, you need to know that they are not permanent. Once the abuse stops and counseling begins, the physical effects usually subside. Bedwetting is a little more difficult to treat than inappropriate sexual arousal because it occurs when you are asleep. But as your world becomes safer that too should diminish.

We have tried to show you that boys are also victims of incest, but they remain silent about the sexual abuse. Although numerous reasons are found for it in the literature, the silence allows the sexual abuse to continue and keeps society in the dark regarding the victimization of boys. If you are a boy who is being sexually abused or you have a male friend who is being sexually abused, you need to *tell someone you trust*. Only then can the victimization be stopped and all children protected.

Chapter 8 describes the incestuous household in even greater detail. Incest is not something that suddenly happens one night when you go to sleep. It generally begins very slowly, and you are tricked into feeling loved and secure with the sexual abuser. We hope the information in Chapter 8 will enable you to protect yourself from an incestuous situation.

The Incestuous Relationship

As we have said, incest does not usually occur dramatically. Most of the time it starts slowly. In the beginning the abuser introduces you to sexual behavior using rewards or threats. That can be as simple as offering you a gift or taking you somewhere. But it can also be denying you a privilege or punishing you for some small misdeed.

Rewards and threats can also be more complex and subtle. If you have been deprived of affection and attention, the physical closeness offered by the abuser affords you at least some sort of affection and special attention. This can be a powerful incentive for you to cooperate.

Sexually abused children find themselves in a no-win situation because the abuser appears to have the final say through his or her older status. The position of the abuser in your household greatly influences your ability to say no even if there is no direct offer of reward or punishment.

Put in this position, you can be easily confused. As a child you were taught to respect, obey, and love older family members. Now, however, one of those trusted persons asks you to do something that you feel is wrong, in exchange for your compliance promising you a "special relationship."

You now have a serious dilemma. If you do not comply with the demands you will not be part of the "special relationship." You may believe that the person will be angry if you refuse. You may feel that he or she will not love you anymore. We all want to feel "special" and loved by the important people in our lives. It is not easy to say no to the people we love. It is also not easy to say no to a person who is in a position of authority over us.

During every war there are instances of soldiers who disagree with orders given to them by their superiors. Some soldiers say no; some do not. Some are tried for *disobeying* the direct orders of their superiors; some are tried for *not disobeying*. Authority is a status that is very hard to challenge, even for adults. If adults have trouble saying no to other adults, it is even more difficult for you to say no to the adults on whom you are dependent.

Once you have complied with the abuser's demands, the sexual abuse often intensifies. It usually begins with genital petting or exhibitionism. Sometimes it goes no further; sometimes it continues through intercourse. Not every situation is the same.

SECRECY

Once the sexual abuse is a reality, the situation in the incestuous household becomes even more complicated. Because incest is not a normal activity within a family, it must be kept secret. The abuser cautions you not to tell anyone else. You may be told that if anyone finds out the abuser will stop loving you or will have to leave the household.

The consequences of revealing the secret might be disguised as threats against you. You might be told that you will be forced to leave the household. You might be told that no one would believe you anyway. As you can see, your dilemma steadily increases. The abuser makes you feel as if it is your responsibility to keep the family together. You feel guilty about keeping secrets and ashamed by the sexual abuse, but you are afraid to do anything for fear of breaking up the household. The offender counts on your sense of loyalty and fear of abandonment to keep the incest a secret. Incest offenders manipulate your behavior and feelings. They take advantage of your dependence, love, trust, and immaturity.

DISCLOSURE

Disclosure is the major fear in an incestuous household. How that disclosure occurs and what happens afterward play a great role in determining your recovery from the incestuous experience. Frequently the disclosure is accidental. It may happen when you confide in a friend who tells a parent. In anger, you may blurt out the story to the nonabusive parent. When the disclosure is accidental, your fear increases. You believe that the abuser's threats will all come true. You wait in anxious silence for the reprisals that are sure to follow. Will you be thrown out of the house? Will the offender be sent to jail, leaving your family with no means of support? Will you be called a liar and be punished accordingly? Will your family reject you?

It is also possible that the disclosure is deliberate. A child who deliberately discloses the abuse is subject to the same fears as one who does so accidentally, but at least he or she is not subject to the anxiety caused by wondering who will find out next. For the first time in this sexually abusive situation, YOU are the more powerful person. If you are believed and action is immediately taken to protect you, then your recovery can begin. The abuse has stopped, and you have been shown that adults can behave in a trustworthy manner. The time for secrecy is over, and you are relieved of the burden of the false responsibility for keeping your family together. If you are not believed, however, the nightmare continues. You discover that the offender's threats are coming true. Then you feel even more isolated, vulnerable, powerless, helpless, and guilty. Now do you see why we said it was a no-win situation?

AFTERMATH

Whether the disclosure was accidental or deliberate, if you were not believed you become more and more anxious. To alleviate anxiety and to put things back the way they were before disclosure, you may recant or take back the story. This is common among incest victims. Another way to alleviate anxiety is to suppress or forget the abuse. This is easier if the abusive behavior stops after disclosure, but it also creates a new tension in the household. Everyone knows what happened whether they openly admitted it or not. Hundreds of questions remain unasked and un- answered. Entire areas of people's lives remain un- discussed. Communication becomes even more limited. You remain confused and hurt and often blame yourself for the new tension in the household as well as for the sexual abuse.

Many cases of incest are uncovered after the victim has become an adult and seeks counseling for some other reason. The simple fact that such victims seek counseling long after the incest has stopped is indicative of the long-range effects that intrafamilial sexual abuse has on children. Some victims do not even remember the sexual abuse until they are adults.

In 1990 four sisters took their father to court for sexual abuse. These women were in their thirties and forties. Two had been hospitalized for psychiatric care. All four had had difficulty forming intimate relationships.

During a psychiatric counseling session one of the sisters remembered that her father, a retired FBI agent and child abuse specialist, had sexually abused her. She then discussed her abuse with her sisters, and they too remembered similar incidents.

At first they agreed simply to talk with their father about their childhood. He denied all the charges, so they decided to take the case to court even though the abuse had happened decades earlier.

Their father believed that they would lose the suit because the statute of limitations had run out, so he continued to deny that he had abused them. Under the law the sisters had a limited time to report the abuse after they reached the age of eighteen. Their lawyers, however, argued their case under a different law. Legally, a victim has two years after discovering that he or she has been injured to report the offense that caused the injury. Because the older sister had repressed the memory of her sexual abuse until she remembered it during counseling, the courts ruled that the sisters could proceed with their suit.

The father lost the case and was ordered to pay millions of dollars in damages to his daughters, although they had only asked for enough money to cover their psychiatric care. He continued to deny the charges and went into hiding. The sisters felt vindicated, however, because many other people had believed them. Although the sisters are still undergoing counseling, they all feel that it was a positive step to confront their father and take him to court. Their chances for recovery have greatly improved.

You may wonder why it took the sisters so long to remember what happened to them. You may wonder how they could ever forget that their father had sexually abused them. A psychiatrist who works with victims of incest says that forgetting is a common defense mechanism. It enables the victim to survive the ordeal, even at a very young age.

When a child is being abused, he or she may be able to block out the experience even while it is happening. We mentioned this dissociation earlier. You may have focused on a spot on the ceiling or a pattern on the wallpaper and just stared at it until you almost went into a trance. That is another type of defense mechanism.

You might also have conflicting emotions about the abusive parent. Children usually love their parents unconditionally. It may be hard for you to accept that a parent would be abusive even while you are being abused. The fact is so horrible that it is not difficult to block out, especially if you never talk about it.

The increase in the number of people who report incestuous experiences is partly because adult women finally remember when they are older. The memory, however, is no less painful than the experience was. The medical profession believes that the sooner incidents of incest are reported and stopped, the easier recovery may be for the victim. Although nothing is easy about the trauma surrounding incest, the sooner you can get help, the better it is. Your recovery depends upon many things, such as: (1) how long the incest had been going on; (2) whether physical force was involved; (3) how many people were involved; (4) whether intercourse occurred; (5) how old you were; and (6) how much support the nonoffending parent gave you.

VICTIMS' REACTIONS

A group of general behaviors and emotions are experienced by many victims of incest. Some appear during or shortly after the incestuous experience. Others are long-term effects that may not be seen or felt until the victim is much older.

It is important to remember that because most cases of incest go unreported, full information is not available. You may experience some, all, or none of these behaviors and feelings. You may experience other feelings. Just as each case differs, so does each child's reaction differ. There is no right or wrong reaction to incest. Take your time as you read the rest of this chapter. As you can see, you are not alone.

Immediate Effects

If you became a victim of incest after starting school, you may find it difficult to concentrate on your schoolwork. You may spend a lot of time worrying about how to avoid the next encounter with your abuser. As a result, your grades may drop and you may fall behind in your work.

Learning takes time and concentration. It is hard enough to pay attention when someone in the next aisle is fooling around, or when the weather is so nice you don't think you can sit in the classroom another minute. How difficult is it to sit in a classroom and listen to a teacher talk about William Shakespeare or factoring equations when you are being sexually abused by a parent? What happens when there is no safe place for you to go after school? Can you concentrate on your schoolwork in an abusive home? Probably not!

Some children become truant; others drop out of school altogether. Victims of incest are in a position where they must deal with a nightmare of a homelife and then try to appear "normal" in the world outside. That is a lot to ask of anyone. The strain of going to school when your grades are falling and you feel you can never catch up can be enough to make anyone quit school.

Children may feel that others can tell what is happening and feel so ashamed that they do not want to be around people. Skipping school may take away the burden of schoolwork, but it does nothing to lessen the abusive atmosphere at home. In fact, it may make matters worse. When you limit yourself to home, you have no opportunity to observe how other people live, to see that people show each other affection in nonsexual ways. Also, dropping out of school limits future opportunities; the dropout fails to learn the educational skills that will lead to better jobs later in life. The only way to achieve money and power is by finishing your education.

Have you ever thought about running away from home? A great many children do run away. However, those children are at great risk for further abuse. They have dropped out of school and usually have no money and no skills. They are easy prey for pimps, drug pushers, and other unsavory persons. Girls tend to run away more often than boys. How would you take care of yourself if you ran away tomorrow? Would you simply be trading one kind of abuse for another?

Some incest victims, usually girls, get married very early in order to get away from home. While that solves the initial problem of getting away from the abuser, marrying young poses its own set of problems. A girl who leaves her parents' house for her husband's with no time in between usually finds herself once again in a dependent situation. This is especially bad if the husband turns out to be an abusive person. Would marrying young eliminate the sexual abuse in your life or increase your chances of becoming a victim of another?

Victims of incest often blame themselves for the abuse. As a way of coping with stress and anxiety in your life, you may develop an eating disorder such as anorexia nervosa (self-starvation) or bulimia (gorging and then throwing up). You may believe that if you had been more attractive this would not have happened. Eating disorders frequently arise out of a desire to change one's body image. Research indicates that you may deliberately do something to make yourself less attractive, such as gaining a lot of weight. You need to realize that your sexual abuse had nothing to do with how you looked. Babies and eighty-year-old women have been sexually abused. The abuse happened to you because you were in a dependent position, not because you were thin or fat, had blue eyes or brown hair.

You may have trouble sleeping or experience frequent nightmares. That is because you are afraid your attacker will sneak up on you. It is also a result of the anxiety produced by the incestuous relationship. However, not all sleep disorders are related to incest; most people experience problems sleeping and have nightmares sometime during their life.

Anger and hostility are other common emotions experienced by sexually abused children. These emotions are directed at the offender and at other members of your family for failing to protect you. The anger and hostility are often manifested by disruptive behavior. You may pick quarrels with classmates or siblings. Often the victim is even angry at himself or herself for not stopping the incest. If you internalize your anger you may try to harm yourself in some way, including abuse of drugs or alcohol. Have you ever experienced shame in relation to incest? Many victims feel shame as well as anger, as if they had some responsibility for the sexual abuse. Guilt often accompanies the experience as well. The guilt tends to be magnified when the abuse is disclosed, especially in situations where the offender is made to leave the home.

Depression is another common immediate effect. It is usually manifested as low self-esteem and feelings of worthlessness. Depression also accompanies feelings of guilt and shame. Everyone becomes depressed to some degree at one time or another. If, however, your depression lingers for a long time and you continue feeling worthless, you need to seek professional help.

Fear is another common emotion, and it comes in various forms. It may be fear of the dark or fear of enclosed places. It could be a fear of men or of women, a fear of water, or even a fear of being alone. Many people have these fears or phobias, but in a victim of incest the fear is more pronounced. If you think your fears may be irrational and they prevent you from living your life to the fullest, you may want to tell someone about them. Just talking to a friend may lessen the fears.

You may feel that you have no value other than as a sexual object. You may also be confused about the difference between sex and affection. That is not surprising since in your experience affection was shown only with sex. But you *are* a valuable human being. There are hundreds of nonsexual ways to show affection, such as giving someone flowers, washing the car unexpectedly, serving breakfast in bed, or paying compliments.

LONG-TERM EFFECTS

Some effects may continue into adulthood, especially if you received inadequate counseling or none. It is impossible to tell how long any of these effects may last, but the sooner you begin professional help, the sooner you will be able to overcome the emotional scars of the incest. You will recover!

SHARED CONCERNS OF INCEST VICTIMS

Not everyone responds the same way to sexual abuse, but most victims have some shared feelings. We shall address some of the more common feelings that you may have. You may be concerned about the physical effects of sexual abuse, especially if you experienced pain. You may wonder if you have been physically injured, if you have suffered permanent damage, if you can have children, or if you have contracted a sexually transmitted disease (STD). If you have any of these concerns, it is important for you to see a doctor. A physical examination can serve two purposes: If there has been physical damage the doctor will be able to begin appropriate treatment. If there has been no physical damage the doctor can put your mind at ease.

You may wonder if anyone else will be able to tell that you have had sex with a relative. The answer is no. There are only two ways anyone will know: first, if you tell them, and second, if you end up in court. Many judges try to protect your anonymity, especially if you are a minor, but it is not always possible.

Is it normal to feel guilty? Yes, but you are *not guilty of anything*. You may feel guilty for several reasons. You may feel you were responsible for the sexual activity. You may feel guilty about having reported the abuse. You may feel guilty because the household has been disrupted by your reporting the abuse. Perhaps the most important lesson you must learn is that *you are not at fault*. No matter what you may think and no matter what anyone else says, you were a dependent person in the household. You were in no position to decide what did or did not happen. The abusive individual is solely to blame.

Children can never be held responsible for initiating sexual activity with an adult or older person. People who tell you that you are responsible do so to avoid being held responsible for their own abusive actions or neglect. You have the right to expect protection from an older person. If you are abused instead of protected, you have a right to report that abuse. Nor are you responsible for what happens *after* you report sexual abuse. The abuser is responsible not only for *initiating* the sexual activity but also for *any and all negative consequences that follow*. The household would not have been disrupted if the older person had not abused his power and position. If you believe that you should have done something to prevent or stop the relationship, remember that nothing you did or did not do justified a sexual approach by a parent or older relative. Adults are expected to be responsible for their own actions. Do not accept the guilt that the abuser should shoulder.

We mentioned earlier that you would be angry. You may feel very angry for a long time. First you may feel angry at the person who abused and exploited you. You may also be angry with other members of your family who failed to protect you. You may feel angry at people around you who have not been as sympathetic as they should have been. You have a right to be angry, but you need to learn how to express your anger safely and in nondestructive ways. Talking with a counselor can help you learn to do that.

There are also therapy groups for incest victims. Often talking with others who have shared the same experiences can help you understand your feelings. There are separate therapy groups for children and adults, and the anonymity of members is protected.

Incest is traumatic because you have been betrayed by someone you trusted. You may feel that you cannot trust anyone. You may feel very alone, especially if you have not received support from other family members. As a result you may feel sad, tired, or sick, which are all symptoms of depression.

Again, a counselor can help you sort out your feelings and recover from depression. What has happened to you has happened to many other people. Some children become so depressed that they mutilate or try to kill themselves. If you feel that way you need to talk to someone immediately. Look in your phone book for the number of the nearest Suicide Hotline. You do not have to give your name, and the person who answers will be able to recommend a therapist to help you.

You may be afraid of what other people may think. Unfortunately, we cannot control what others think about us. If some of your friends are acting "different" around you, you may want to ask them directly what they are thinking. Committing incest is not the only taboo; some people are unable even to talk about it. Try not to let what other people say undermine your self-confidence. You must keep repeating to yourself that you were the victim and had no control over the situation. In time, curiosity will die down and people may begin behaving more sympathetically.

You may have a negative image of your physical self. You may think that you are ugly, too fat, or too short. Sometimes this kind of thinking can lead to eating disorders. Take a good look at yourself in the mirror and try to be objective. Incest victims frequently develop a false negative image and sometimes need another person to refute that image. Consult with your school nurse or physical education teacher if you think you need to lose or gain weight. They can help you safely improve your health and fitness level.

One of the best therapies available for incest victims is talking with other victims. Sharing the experience with others who know what you have gone through is an important step in understanding what happened to you. Look in the phone book for a listing for Parents United or Sons and Daughters United. Ask your school counselor for the names of groups that could help you. These organizations will help you realize that your life has *not* been ruined forever.

You may feel confused about your relationship with your mother. Listen to Allison's words and see if you can identify with her:

"I couldn't make up my mind whether I was angry or ashamed. I was mad at my mother, because I felt she should have known what was going on. I felt she should have protected me from my dad. Even though my dad worked so hard to make sure it was a secret and that Mom was never home when it happened, I felt she should have figured it out without me having to tell her. Other times I couldn't even look her in the eye, I was so ashamed. There I was sleeping with her husband when she was out working to pay for the things I wanted. I felt like the other woman. She loved my dad so much. So many times I wanted to tell her but I just couldn't."

You may feel different or uncomfortable or "older" around your peers. While your girlfriends are discussing boys or their first French kiss, you may already have had sex with a family member. Incest robs you of your natural social development. By having experienced sex while your friends are only beginning to explore their sexuality, you may feel isolated and alone. Talking with other incest victims or a counselor can help. You are not the only child who has been victimized by a trusted adult. Have you ever thought that one of your friends may also be a victim and just can't talk about it yet? You may be able to help your friend come to terms with his or her own abuse.

You may feel confused about your feelings toward the person who abused you. It is possible to feel anger and love at the same time. You may love the offender but hate what that person did to you. It is important not to confuse what you wish was and what really is. Children give their love indiscriminately, but as they get older they learn to be more selective. You need to learn to put a value on yourself. Sometimes we confuse love with dependence. There is nothing wrong with disliking someone who mistreats us.

THINGS TO REMEMBER

A growing number of groups are available for people who have been victims of incest. The following are some of the things they say to one another in trying to learn to cope with their experiences:

> You have a right to your own body.
> You have a right to your own feelings, beliefs, opinions, and thoughts.
> You have a right to say yes.
> You have a right to say no.
> You have a right to ask questions.

You have a right to accurate sexual information.
You have a right to be in control of your own sexual
  experiences.
You have a right to dignity and respect.
You have a right to have your needs and wants
  respected by others.
You have a right to personal space.
You have a right to personal time.
You have a right to expect honesty from others.
You have a right to make friends and be comfortable
  around other people.
You have a right to be in a nonabusive environment.

As you can see, incest victims share a wide variety of
symptoms, feelings, and concerns. You may have been
able to identify with several of them. On the other hand,
you may be experiencing very different reactions to your
sexual abuse. There is no right or wrong response to incest.
However, the next chapter may give you the courage to
take the first step in dealing with the abuse.

CHAPTER ◇ 9

Whom Do You Tell?

The first thing that must be done to begin recovering from an incestuous experience is to stop the abuse by breaking the silence. As long as the abuse continues, the emotional and psychological harm deepens. If you feel that you are not in a position to stop the incest by yourself, you must tell someone else. If you are not ready to go directly to the authorities, go to an adult whom you trust and who you think will believe you. Make a list of people you trust, including people with whom you have a fairly good relationship. They can be relatives or friends, a teacher or your school counselor, a religious leader.

The first person you choose may not believe you. It is impossible to predict how anyone else will act in a situation, especially one as complicated and harmful as incest. Talking about incest seems to be as much of a taboo as committing incest. Nevertheless, you must keep telling your story until someone listens to you and acts on your behalf. If the first person you tell does not believe you, don't give up. Try someone else. It may be hard to talk about your experience, especially if the first person you tell doesn't believe you. Do *not* start second-guessing yourself. You know what happened to you.

TELLING YOUR MOTHER

Telling your mother would seem the most normal thing to do if you have been sexually abused by a relative. Unfortunately that is not always the case, especially when the abuser is your father. Many children are already angry at their mother for not having prevented the abuse in the first place. Professionals disagree on whether most mothers are even aware of the abuse. Some say that the mother almost always knows what has been going on. At the very least, they say, she suspects it but is unwilling to deal with the situation. Unfortunately, suspicions are not always enough to confront someone with a crime as serious as incest. Sometimes, too, when a mother has suspicions and asks her daughter if "something is going on," the daughter denies it. If all the mother has are suspicions and she wrongly accuses the father, she risks seriously damaging her relationship with her husband.

Research has also shown that some mothers set up their daughters for the incestuous relationship by dressing them in suggestive clothing or telling them to "take care of Daddy" while they are absent. The research does not tell us how frequently this happens, but once is too often.

Still others question how mothers are supposed to know when the relationship is kept secret and usually occurs when she is out of the home. A mother may feel an uncomfortable tension when her husband and daughter are together but honestly not be able to pinpoint the source of her discomfort.

The fact is that some mothers are quite aware of what is going on but pretend not to notice for fear of disrupting the family or losing economic support. On the other hand, some mothers are totally unaware of what is happening. Each child's situation is different, and every mother is different. Only you can decide whether you can tell your mother.

What to Expect When You Tell Your Mother

It is impossible to tell ahead of time whether a mother will be supportive or not. Incest, although initially involving only the offending adult and the victimized child, affects many people. Incest, by definition, involves family members. If the offender is your father, he is also your mother's husband. If he is your grandfather or uncle, he is also your mother's or your father's father or brother. If the offender is your father, your mother may feel she has little to gain by believing you. If she openly believes you and acts to make her husband leave, she risks losing the economic or emotional security he provides. If you were in your mother's situation, would it be hard for you to believe your own child was being sexually abused by your spouse? Why, or why not?

It is important to remember that no matter what happens, you did not set the stage. *The offender is responsible for anything and everything that happens*. Do not start blaming yourself by saying, "If only I had said no." Saying no might have cost your life.

Remember why you were unable to stop the incest from occurring. Remember that you are a child and the offender is an adult. Perhaps the most important thing to remember is that you are not responsible in any way. You are the victim. Children are not born with the social skills necessary to survive in the adult world. One of the purposes of the family is to nurture the child and teach him or her the skills we all need to mature and interact with one another in a responsible manner. No child can be held responsible for the behavior of any adult. No child can be held responsible for the consequences of an adult's behavior.

Your mother may react with a great deal of support and move immediately to protect you, but that is an ideal situation. If you feel uncomfortable telling your mother, tell someone else.

TELLING YOUR FATHER

Although the vast majority of victims are girls and most offenders are male, your father may be the person to tell about the sexual abuse. You may already be angry at your father for not preventing the abuse in the first place. Aren't fathers big and strong? Don't we expect them to protect us from all harm?

Little research has been done on whether or not fathers are aware of the abuse. Some professionals say that the father almost always knows. Others disagree, believing the stereotype that men are not as perceptive as women, and therefore fathers may suspect something but not act until the evidence is overwhelming. Notice how similar the reactions of your mother and father may be.

How is your father supposed to know about the incestuous behavior if it has been kept a secret? The abuse probably occurred while your father was not at home. Although he may feel an uncomfortable tension when his wife and son are together, he may honestly be unable to pinpoint the source of his discomfort.

Odds are that some fathers are quite aware of what is going on but pretend not to notice for fear of disrupting the family or losing emotional support. But other fathers are totally unaware of what is happening. If your parents are divorced or separated and you live with your father, he may be totally unaware of what is happening to you at your mother's home. Your mother's boyfriend/lover may be the abusive adult. Each child's situation is different, and only you can decide whether you can tell your father.

What to Expect When You Tell Your Father

Each father will respond differently. Some fathers will be supportive and stop the abuse immediately. Because men earn more money than women, fathers who do not put an end to the incest tend to be emotionally weak rather than fearful of economic loss. However, some fathers will deny that incest is occurring and do nothing to stop the abuse.

It is impossible to tell ahead of time which fathers will be supportive and which will not. Incest affects all members of the family, not just the offending adult and the victimized child. If the offender is your mother, she is also your father's wife. If it is the grandmother or aunt, it is also your father's mother or sister. If the offender is your mother, your father may think that he has everything to lose if he believes you. Once he believes you, he must send his wife away, which means that he has lost her emotional security.

If you were in your father's situation, what kind of evidence would you need to suspect incest? If you asked your child whether anything was going on and your child said no, would you confront your spouse about your suspicions anyway? Why, or why not?

Fortunately, some fathers react with a great deal of support and move quickly to protect you. But that is the ideal situation. If you feel uncomfortable telling your father, tell someone else. Eventually someone will listen to you and believe you. Keep in mind that *you are the victim, not the offender*.

TELLING OTHER ADULTS

Unfortunately there is no way to predict how anyone will act when you say you have been sexually abused. Nevertheless, you must tell someone. If your mother does not respond well or you are afraid to talk to her, go to a relative. You may be able to tell your grandmother or an aunt. The most important step in recovering from the trauma of incest is to break the silence. You have been carrying a heavy burden alone for too long. Once you tell someone, you will begin to feel a little better because you now have someone who can protect you from the abuser.

Teacher

A teacher may be the easiest person to tell. You spend almost eight hours a day at school and have contact with several teachers. Can you identify your favorite teacher right now? What qualities does this person have that make him or her so easy to talk to?

There are several different ways to tell your teacher. First, if you are afraid to do so face to face, you may want to write a short note and leave it on the teacher's desk. Second, you may be able to write about the sexual abuse in one of your assignments. That will give your teacher a chance to write a note back to you. A third way, but a little harder for your teacher to figure out, is to draw a picture of the sexual abuse. The very best way to tell your teacher is simply in a private meeting after school. That gives both of you plenty of time to ask questions and determine the best course of action. You have the right to decide what you want to happen and how it happens.

Every state has some type of Child Protection Act that teachers and schools are bound to follow. You need to know that once you tell your teacher or the school counselor, he or she is bound by law to report it to the appropriate state agency. Remember that these agencies are responsible for protecting you when your family is unable or unwilling to do so.

Counselors

Most school counselors have training in helping children with a wide assortment of problems. Remember that if you are a victim of incest you are not in a unique situation. If your counselor performs his or her job well, he or she will be very supportive. When the time is right your counselor will be able to direct you to where you can get additional counseling and meet other children who share your secret of sexual abuse. As a representative of the school, your counselor will make every attempt to protect you from further harm both at home and at school.

Religious Leaders

You may feel most comfortable telling a religious person at your place of worship. Be aware that although your religious leader is a person of God, he or she is also a human being. As human beings, religious leaders are subject to the same flaws as the rest of us. *If you are not believed, do not give up.* Do not tell yourself that if your church leader doesn't believe you, you must be guilty. You know that is not true, so you must keep trying.

*   *   *

Finding the right person to tell about your sexual abuse is not an easy task. It may take several attempts before you are believed and someone helps you. Most people believe that family privacy is sacred except in extraordinary circumstances. This sanctity of the family is one of the major factors that have kept incest and sexual abuse a secret for so long. It was not until the 1960s that researchers began writing and talking about child sexual abuse. Being sexually abused *is an extraordinary circumstance*. Therefore, if you don't feel comfortable telling a person you know, Chapter 10 addresses how you can tell an agency.

Telling an Outside Agency

Treatment for incest victims and their families varies from agency to agency and from state to state. The first thing that usually happens when incest is reported to an outside agency is that the agency moves to protect you from further abuse. Many states require that you be removed immediately from the household if the abuser is also in the household. Usually you must remain out of the home until the offender leaves or admits his abusive behavior and agrees to treatment. That may seem like punishing you, but the first priority of any social service agency is to remove you to safety. Studies have shown that incest seldom occurs only once. Even if the abuser promises to stop his behavior, it usually continues. If you were able to protect yourself and were not in a dependent position, the abuse would not have occurred in the first place. Therefore someone must protect you if your family has not.

Kerry's Story

Kerry's father began abusing her when she was nine years old. He warned her not to tell anyone, that this was their "special secret." The abuse continued for three years until one day she told her best friend, Alice, about it. Alice was upset by what Kerry was going through and asked her mother what she could do to help. Alice's mother called the Department of Social Services in their area. When the people from Social Services showed up at Kerry's house, her father was very angry. He denied that he had been sexually abusing his daughter and said she was making the story up. Kerry's mother also said that nothing was going on. When the investigator asked Kerry if she had been sexually abused, she did not know what to say. She was afraid that if she said yes her father would become even angrier. She was also afraid that she would hurt her mother. So Kerry recanted and said there must have been a mistake. The investigators went away.

That night Kerry heard her parents arguing. It was a long time before she was able to fall asleep. The next day her mother asked her if her father had been abusing her. Again, Kerry denied it. Kerry's mother became very angry and called her a "lying troublemaker." For weeks no one in the house really talked to anyone else. Although Kerry was upset by the tension in the house, she was relieved that her father was staying away from her.

One afternoon several months later, while her mother was out shopping, Kerry's father approached her again. When she started to resist he told her that it wouldn't do any good because no one had believed her the first time, not even her mother.

*   *   *

Why did Kerry deny the abuse when the Social Services people asked her? Are you surprised that her parents argued about it that night? What was Kerry afraid of when her mother questioned her about the abuse? If you were Kerry, would you have told your mother the first time she asked you?

Notice that the incest *did not stop* even though Kerry's father knew that both his wife and the Department of Social Services suspected him. Now do you see why you may have to be removed from your home if the abuser denies the incestuous behavior? What should Kerry do now that her father has approached her again? Should she tell her mother that she had been afraid to admit the sexual abuse, or should she call the Department of Social Services? Kerry is right no matter which decision she makes. As long as she tells someone that she is being sexually abused and sticks to the facts, she has made the right decision. Would this be a hard decision for you to make? Of course it would! Telling the truth is not always an easy decision, even for adults, but it is the *only* decision.

When you remain in a home with an abuser who denies the abuse, you are not only in danger of further sexual abuse but also of emotional abuse. When other family members deny that the abuse occurred you may start second-guessing yourself, especially when they continue to tell you that the report was untrue.

In addition, family members may pressure you to retract the report. You may be made to feel guilty for the disruption in the family. Someone must be available to give you positive emotional support. The people who work in outside agencies are trained to help you. They care about your safety and well-being.

When a case of incest has been reported and your father is removed from the house, he may call you and appeal to your emotional relationship in an effort to get you to change your story. You may feel torn because you have been taught to love and respect your father. Also things may not be running so smoothly in the household with your father gone. No matter how hard it is, know that you made the right decision.

Another scenario may be that you have been removed from the home and are homesick and lonely. Many people, including adults, stay in relationships that are abusive and painful because they are used to them. It is difficult to face change, so it is understandable that children frequently change their minds about reporting.

If you are a victim of incest, remaining in an abusive household affects not only your life now but how you will deal with situations later in life. It is extremely important to get away from the abuse. If you can avoid the pitfalls of recanting, the road to recovery is in sight.

Once you are under the protection of a state agency, you are usually given therapy to help you cope with what has happened. In therapy you are again reassured that the abuse was beyond your control. Group therapy allows you to exchange feelings and experiences with other incest victims. This sharing seems to be very effective in helping you understand what happened. It is also beneficial to hear how other children coped with their experiences.

Incest affects the functioning of the entire family, and other family members are expected to join in therapy. This can be very painful, especially if you come face to face with your abuser. Therapists have a variety of techniques to make this easier. Although they may use confrontational techniques, they usually prefer role-reversal techniques. In a role reversal you would take the part of the abuser and say what you believe the abuser would say or think. This method can be especially helpful in letting other family members know how you perceived the abuse. It also allows you and other family members to express anger and other feelings in a controlled atmosphere. Can you think of things you would like to say to the abuser in this safe setting? Would you feel better if you could express your anger? Would you enjoy being in a *powerful* rather than a powerless position? Now you can see why therapy is an essential part of the healing process. You are finally regaining control of your own life.

GOING TO COURT

When a report of child sexual abuse is made and the offender denies the charge, the case has to go before a judge. Unfortunately this experience can be almost as traumatic for you as the incest. If you have to go to court, you must be prepared to expect certain things.

First, you will be examined by doctors for physical evidence of sexual abuse. Some children find this extremely humiliating and impersonal, but it can provide important evidence for the trial.

Second, you may be questioned by people from the district attorney's office, the Department of Social Services, or even the police department. It may seem to you that they act as if they don't believe you, or what happened is your fault. If that is so, try to remember that many people are uncomfortable talking about incest. Not everyone is able to deal with the fact that parents sexually abuse their children.

It is important to tell yourself that you are going through all this so that you can get on with your life without any more sexual abuse. Some agencies are more sensitive than others. In some areas of the country your testimony is videotaped so that you do not have to repeat it so often.

Going to court makes many children feel humiliated, embarrassed, and even more isolated than they did before the incest was reported. The purpose, however, is to end the abuse once and for all. Before recovery can begin, *the abuse must be stopped.*

Telling an outside agency may be easier than telling someone you know, for several reasons. First, they have dealt with thousands of these situations, and they will believe you. Second, most of the people working in the Department of Social Services have received special training in assisting you. Third, because they do not know you or the abuser, they will not be judgmental the way a family member, friend, or other adult might be.

You cannot change the fact that the incest happened, but you can change your feelings of powerlessness. Rather than just reacting to the abuse, you can become proactive and empower yourself. If you are not ready to report the abuse, Chapter 11 addresses how to be assertive and offers avoidance skills that you can incorporate into your daily living.

Avoidance Skills and

Assertiveness

HOW TO AVOID BECOMING A VICTIM

One of the first things you must learn is to say no. Your body is your property; it does not belong to your parents, your grandparents, your aunt or your uncle, your brother or your sister. Only you have the right to say who will touch your body. Often saying no is sufficient. One of the reasons an adult turns to you for sexual gratification is the belief that you will not refuse.

By saying no you let the adult know that your body is your own property and that you are aware that what he or she is attempting to do is wrong. No one has a right to touch your body in a way that makes you uncomfortable. No one has a right to make you touch someone else's body in a way that makes you uncomfortable. You have a right to control what happens to your body.

As soon as a relative touches you in a way that makes you uncomfortable or makes a suggestion that you feel uneasy about, tell someone. If saying no does not stop the behavior, telling someone else about the situation usually does.

If a relative is making you uncomfortable and you are in a room alone together, begin talking loudly so that people in other parts of the house will hear you. Remember that the adult who is engaging in sexually abusive behavior knows that what he or she is doing is wrong. The risk that someone else in the household may witness abuse will usually stop the abuser.

If you are alone in a room with someone who is making you uncomfortable, leave the room. People are often afraid to react negatively to another person, especially a relative. Remember again that the adult who is making you uncomfortable knows that what he or she is doing is wrong. Chances are you are not the only one who feels uncomfortable with that person. *It is better to be rude than to become a victim.*

HOW TO STOP INCEST

One of the most effective ways to stop incest is to report it to the authorities. Unfortunately, that is easier said than done. Many children fear outside intervention as much as they fear the continuing abuse. All too often the abuser has threatened that if anyone finds out the household will be disrupted, or you will be made to leave the home, or the offender will be put in jail.

If you are unable to tell a trusted adult or to go to the authorities at this time, there are avoidance strategies that you can use. Start with the strategy that is easiest for you to implement first. If one does not work in your situation, change to a different one. It may be that several strategies combined will stop the abuse, or none may work in your situation. Don't give up ! If none of these works, it is time to tell a trusted adult.

The first thing to do is try to avoid being alone with the offender. The easiest offender to avoid is one who does not live with you. If it is your grandfather or an uncle, make up excuses for not visiting that person's home. If the abuse occurs when the offender visits your home, try to avoid being alone with him or her or arrange to be somewhere else during the person's visits.

If the offender is someone in your home such as your father, your mother, or your brother, lock your door at night. If you do not have a lock, buy a lock and put it on. A simple padlock can be attached by screwing braces to the inside of your door and door frame. The offender will know why you are putting a lock on your door, and chances are he will be unwilling to make an issue of it.

Push furniture against your door at night. To get into your room the offender will have to make a lot of noise, which will wake others in the house. He probably won't want to explain to other family members why he was trying to get into your room. Can you think of an acceptable reason why someone would need to be in your room at 1 am?

Never shower when you are alone in the house with the offender. You are in a vulnerable position when you are naked. If you must, make certain you lock the bathroom door. Call a friend and ask him or her to check on you in fifteen minutes. Ask your friend to come over if you don't personally talk to him or her on the phone. Friends take care of each other, and this is no imposition. Wouldn't you do it for him or her?

Whenever the offender approaches you, make a lot of noise. Even if other people in the household are aware of the abuse but ignoring it, it is not likely that they can ignore loud noises or shouting. However, if you are in a household with an offender and you yell and scream and no one responds, you are at great risk for continued and multiple abuse. If this is how you live, you must report the abuse at once. *Your life may be in danger.*

It may be possible to recognize the times when the abuse occurs, such as when the offender has been drinking or on nights when other people in the household are not at home. It is imperative for you to arrange to be somewhere else during that time. Go to a friend's house or invite a friend over to your house. Rarely is pretending to be asleep a sufficient deterrent. It is best to remove yourself from the potentially abusive situation.

We recognize that not everyone is in a position to follow these suggestions. In some households the level of physical violence is so high that any attempt to protect yourself will result in an escalation of the abuse. We are also fully aware that some children are virtual prisoners in their own homes and are unable to escape when a potentially abusive situation arises.

If you have decided not to report the abuse, think about that decision again. Think about how much time and energy are going into avoiding the offender. Think about how much emotional turmoil you live with by being a victim of incest. Think about how lonely it is not being able to tell anyone.

Epilogue

Sexual abuse happens to children of every socioeconomic level, culture, race, religion, and gender. As we mentioned in Chapter 1, one in three girls and one in four boys will be sexually abused by their eighteenth birthday. Using even conservative estimates, researchers predict that approximately 210,000 new cases of sexual abuse occur each year.

If you have read this book from cover to cover you may be wondering whether you or a close friend are a victim of sexual abuse. Incestuous behavior and sexual abuse include a wide range of activities, which occur in a progressive manner. If you are still unsure whether or not you have been victimized, answer the following questions quickly and honestly:

WERE YOU EVER...   **YES**   **NO**

Exposed to nudity at an inappropriate age,   ____   ____
    place, or time?
Bathed in a way that made you   ____   ____
    uncomfortable?
Watched while you were getting undressed?   ____   ____
Touched in sexual areas?   ____   ____
Made to watch sexual acts or look at sexual   ____   ____
    parts?
Shown sexual movies?   ____   ____

Forced to pose for suggestive or sexual photographs?	___	___
Forced to listen to sexual talk?	___	___
Told that all you were good for was sex?	___	___
Held, kissed, or fondled in a way that made you uncomfortable?	___	___
Masturbated by an older person?	___	___
Forced to perform oral sex on an adult or sibling?	___	___
Raped or penetrated by a finger or object?	___	___
Forced to have anal sex with an adult or sibling?	___	___
Involved in child prostitution or pornography?	___	___
Forced to have vaginal intercourse with an adult or sibling?	___	___
Physically or sexually tortured?	___	___

If you answered yes to any of these questions, the odds are you have been victimized by a family member or trusted adult who had power over you. However, you may have answered no to all the questions but still feel somehow uneasy and violated. We call this feeling your *sixth sense*. If you have an inner feeling that something isn't right, trust that feeling and listen to your inner voice. In the vast majority of incest cases the victim thinks she has been abused and later confirms her suspicions.

Regardless of your age or circumstances, there is never an excuse for sexual abuse. The responsibility for the abuse lies solely with the adult or older individual. YOU WERE NOT RESPONSIBLE FOR THE SEXUAL ABUSE. Whether or not you fought off the sexual advances is irrelevant. You were powerless over your abuser. As a child you did not have the skills or power to protect yourself.

Whether or not you had any sexual response is also irrelevant. You were an unwilling victim who did not have the capacity to consent. You may have been physically coerced or emotionally manipulated into the sexual behavior because you needed affection and attention. If these basic needs were not offered to you in nonsexual ways, you tried to obtain them in whatever way you could. Even though you may not have understood what was happening, the abuser did.

Whether or not you received any sexual pleasure is once again irrelevant. The human body is a marvelous machine with numerous systems that we cannot control. When we eat a sandwich, our stomach digests the sandwich. No matter how hard we try, we cannot stop our stomach from digesting the sandwich. When our body is touched and we are sexually stimulated, the sexual response cycle is put into motion. We can no more stop our body from sexually responding than we can stop the digestive process. That does not mean that you wanted to be sexually abused. It simply means that when your abuser stimulated your body it responded appropriately. Your body did not betray you; the abusive individual betrayed his or her position of power over you.

If you have discovered that you are in an abusive situation, you need to stop the abuse by breaking the silence. We have tried to give you an overview of the abuser, the victim, and the incestuous household. We have recommended people and places that you can contact for help. An explanation of the legal system should have removed some of your fear about what to expect once you report the abuse. You need to accept the fact that while THE ABUSER ALONE IS RESPONSIBLE FOR THE

ABUSE, YOU ALONE ARE RESPONSIBLE FOR YOUR
RECOVERY. We wish you well on your journey and pray
that you act immediately on your own behalf. Take us with
you on your journey and you will never be alone again.

Glossary

covert incest   Suggestive sexual behavior toward another family member with no physical contact.

dysfunctional family   One that is not working, that has something wrong.

empathy   The ability to experience someone else's feelings yourself.

family of origin/the original family   Mother, father, brothers, and sisters.

incest   Any sexual activity between family members who are too closely related to be married.

intrafamilial   Between members of the same family.

pedophile   A person who enjoys sex with young children.

promiscuous   Having many sexual partners.

sexual abuse   Any sexual activity for the gratification of an older person between an older person and a much younger person.

STD (sexually transmitted disease)   A disease contracted from another person during sex; examples: gonorrhea; AIDS; syphylis; herpes simplex 2.

surrogate/substitute/father surrogate   A parent's boyfriend, brother, cousin; any older male in the household who assumes the duties and responsibilities of a natural father.

taboo   Traditionally forbidden.

transient   Temporary.

Appendix: Where to Obtain Help

CRISIS COUNSELING

More than 300 agencies nationwide are affiliated with the Family Service Association of America. These agencies offer individual and family counseling at low cost as well as a variety of other family services.

For the agency nearest you, check your phone directory under the following listings:

Family Service Association
Council for Community Service
County Health Department
Counseling Clinic
Mental Health Clinic
United Fund

or call the New York Office at (212) 674-6100.

For immediate help, call:

CHILD ABUSE/FAMILY VIOLENCE HOTLINE:
                      1 (800) 422-4453

DRUG ABUSE HOTLINE: 1 (800) 548-3008
     in Arizona: 1 (800) 874-9070

GLENBEIGH FOOD ADDICTIONS HOTLINE:
                      1 (800) 4A-BINGE

ADDITIONAL LISTINGS IN YOUR PHONEBOOK

Crisis Center   Suicide Prevention Center
Help Line   Victims Crisis Center
Adolescent Clinic   Hotline

Usually your phone directory will have several hotline numbers for your area inside the front cover.

WHERE TO WRITE FOR MORE INFORMATION

Institute for the Community as Extended Family
(Parents United, Daughters and Sons United)
P.O. Box 952
San Jose, CA 95108

National Center for the Prevention of Child Abuse and Neglect
1205 Oneida Street
Denver, CO 80220

Bibliography

Bass, E., and Davis, L. *The Courage to Heal*. New York: Harper and Row, 1988.

Bronson, C. *Growing Through the Pain*. New York: A Prentice Hall/Parkside Recovery Book, 1989.

Bruckner, D. F., and Johnson, P. E. "Treatment for Adult Victims of Childhood Sexual Abuse." *Social Casework: The Journal of Contemporary Social Work*, February 1987, 81–7.

Campbell, P. *Sex Guides: Books and Films about Sexuality for Young Adults*. New York: Garland Publishing, 1986.

Cleveland, D. *Incest: The Story of Three Women*. Lexington, MA: D.C. Heath And Co., 1986.

Crewdson, J. *By Silence Betrayed: Sexual Abuse of Children in America*. Boston: Little, Brown and Co., 1988.

Finkelhor, D. *A Sourcebook on Child Sexual Abuse*. Beverly Hills: Sage Publications, 1986.

Forward, S., and Buck, C. *Betrayal of Innocence: Incest and Its Devastation*. New York: Penguin Books, 1983.

Gagliano, C. K. "Group Treatment for Sexually Abused Girls." *Social Casework: The Journal of Contemporary Social Work*, February 1987, 102–108.

Geiser, R. *Hidden Victims: The Sexual Abuse of Children*. Boston: Beacon Press, 1979.

Haden, D. C. *Out of Harm's Way: Readings on Child Sexual Abuse, Its Prevention and Treatment*. Phoenix, AZ: Oryx Press, 1986.

Halpern, J. "Family Therapy in Father-Son Incest: A Case Study." *Social Casework: The Journal of Contemporary Social Work*, February 1987, 88–93.

Haugaard, J., and Reppucci, N. *The Sexual Abuse of Children.* San Francisco: Jossey-Bass, 1981.

Hodson, D., and Skeen, P. "Child Sexual Abuse: A Review of Research and Theory with Implications for Family Life Educators." *Family Relations.* 36, 1987, 215–21.

Hyde, M. O. *Sexual Abuse: Let's Talk About It.* Philadelphia: Westminster Press, 1984.

Kilgore, L. C. "Effect of Early Child Sexual Abuse on Self and Ego Development." *Social Casework: The Journal of Contemporary Social Work,* April 1988, 224–30

Kosof, A. *Incest: Families in Crisis.* New York: Franklin Watts, 1985.

Landes, R. S. "Child Sexual Abuse: Implications for Health Education." *The Eta Sigma Gamma Monograph Series,* (9)1. July, 1991, 14–21.

Meiselman, K. C. *Incest: A Psychological Study of Causes and Effects with Treatment Recommendations.* San Francisco: Jossey-Bass, Inc., 1978.

National Center on Child Abuse and Neglect. "Research Symposium on Child Sexual Abuse." Washington, DC: U.S. Department of Health and Human Services, 1988.

Nelson, M., and Clark, K. *Preventing Child Sexual Abuse.* Santa Cruz, CA: Network Publications, 1986.

Orten, J. D., and Rich, L. L. "A Model of Assessment of Incestuous Families." *Social Casework: The Journal of Contemporary Social Work,* December 1988, 611–9.

Pierce, L. H. "Father-Son Incest: Using the Literature to Guide Practice." *Social Casework: The Journal of Contemporary Social Work,* February 1987, 67–74.

Renvoize, J. *Incest: A Family Pattern.* London: Routledge & Kegan Paul Ltd., 1982.

Riggs, R. "Incest: The School's Role." *The Journal of School Health,* 1982, 52, 365–70.

Rosenberg, M. "Adult Behaviors that Reflect Childhood Incest." *Medical Aspects of Human Sexuality,* May 1988, 114–24.

Russell, D.E.H. *The Secret Trauma: Incest in the Lives of Girls and Women*. New York: Basic Books, Inc., 1986.

Sebold, J. "Indicators of Child Sexual Abuse in Males." *Social Casework: The Journal of Contemporary Social Work*, February 1987, 75–80.

Sgroi. S. M. *Handbook of Clinical Intervention in Child Sexual Abuse*. Lexington, MA: D.C. Heath and Co., 1982.

Smith, H., and Israel, E. "Sibling Incest: A Study of the Dynamics of 25 Cases." *Child Abuse and Neglect: The International Journal*, 11, 1987, 101–8.

Stark, E. "The Unspeakable Family Secret." *Psychology Today*, May 1984, 42–6.

Summit, R. "The Child Sexual Accommodation Syndrome." *Child Abuse and Neglect: The International Journal*, 11, 1987, 177–93.

Vander Mey, B. "The Sexual Victimization of Male Children: A Review of Previous Research." *Child Abuse and Neglect: The International Journal*, 12, 1988, 61–72.

For Further Reading

Allen, Charlotte Vale. *Daddy's Girl*. New York: Wyndham Books, 1980.

Armstrong, Louise. *Kiss Daddy Goodnight: A Speakout on Incest*. New York: Hawthorn Press, 1978.

Bauer, Marion Dane. *Foster Child*. New York: Seabury Press, 1977.

Brady, Katherine. *Father's Days: A True Story of Incest*. New York: Dell Publishing, 1981.

Butler, Sandra Day. *Conspiracy of Silence: The Trauma of Incest*. San Francisco: New Glide Publications, 1978.

Colao, Florence, and Hosanksy, Tamar. *Your Children Should Know*. New York: Bobbs-Merrill, 1983.

Chetin, Helen. *Frances Ann Speaks Out: My Father Raped Me*. Berkeley: New Seed Press, 1977.

Daugherty, Lynn B. *Why Me? Help for Victims of Child Sexual Abuse (Even If They Are Adults Now)*. Racine, WI: Mother Courage Press, 1984.

Hyde, Margaret O. *My Friend Wants to Run Away*. New York: McGraw Hill, 1979.

————. *Sexual Abuse: Let's Talk About It*. Philadelphia: Westminster Press, 1984.

Hermes, Patricia. *A Solitary Secret*. New York: Harcourt Brace, 1985.

Morrison, Toni. *The Bluest Eye*. New York: Washington Square Press, 1970.

Index